Will Shortz's

MIND GAMES

100 ALPHABET RIDDLES

Will Shortz's

MIND GAMES

100 ALPHABET RIDDLES

WILL SHORTZ

ST. MARTIN'S GRIFFIN
NEW YORK

www.stmartins.com

ISBN-13: 978-0-312-38273-5
ISBN-10: 0-312-38273-1

First Edition: August 2008

10 9 8 7 6 5 4 3 2 1

Introduction

Welcome to *Alphabet Riddles,* a collection of puzzle-quizzes in which all the answers in each particular set have some shared spelling constraint.

For example, in a puzzle featuring two-word phrases with the initials F. F., the answers might include FISH FILET, FEATURE FILM, FANCY FREE, etc.

I've been creating alphabet riddles off and on for NPR's *Weekend Edition Sunday* for more than twenty years. There seems to be no end of alphabetical constraints. Many of the puzzles in this book have been drawn from my weekly NPR segment. The clues have been polished and updated, as necessary. Usually more examples are included here than I had time to use on the air.

I've also created alphabet riddles for TV appearances, such as in 2003 on *The Daily Show* with Jon Stewart (using J. S.) and in 2005 on *The Late Show With David Letterman* (using D. L.). Occasionally I've created these puzzles as birthday presents for friends or for other special occasions. This book includes some of these, too.

Since alphabet riddles are designed to be presented orally,

they're ideal to play out loud with family and friends. Try them on a car trip or while sitting around the family room. You can also do them alone, though, either with a pencil or without.

I think it's safe to say nobody will answer all the questions correctly to all the puzzles in this book. For one thing the tests of knowledge are too diverse. But you will assuredly know most of the answers, so don't give up too soon.

As always, the answers appear in the back.

—Will Shortz

Will Shortz's

MIND GAMES

100 ALPHABET RIDDLES

1. P'S AND CLUES

Each answer is a hyphenated word or a familiar two-word phrase that starts and ends with the letter P.
Ex. It holds sheets together: *Paper clip*

1. Store with three gold balls by the door _____
2. London fog is said to resemble this _____
3. Product from Ruffles _____
4. Beat with the butt of a gun _____
5. Sinus problem during a cold _____
6. It flies a skull and crossbones flag _____
7. It goes in the corner of an envelope _____
8. Meat item often served with applesauce _____
9. It's used to open most soft drink cans _____
10. Kind of truck _____
11. Actions taken by someone who's carried away with his authority _____
12. Floor light popular during the '60s and '70s _____
13. Item tossed into the kitty _____
14. Time to refuel during an auto race _____
15. Abba or the Beatles, for example _____

2. DOUBLE CURVE

Each answer is a familiar two-word phrase or name with the initials S. S.

Ex. Imaginary creature of sailing lore: *Sea serpent*

1. Monthly check for the elderly _____
2. Children's game of imitation _____
3. Something you put on Chinese or Japanese food _____
4. When the biggest football game of the year is held _____
5. ESP _____
6. Central American capital _____
7. Store receipt _____
8. World War II soldier in the comics _____
9. Catchphrase for condom use _____
10. One minute _____
11. *Fiddler on the Roof* song _____
12. The earth's location _____
13. Educational TV show for children _____
14. Overturned jail term _____
15. Hero or hoagie _____
16. Dashiell Hammett detective _____
17. Rachel Carson book on the environment _____
18. BMW or Rolex watch, e.g. _____
19. Emphatic "yes," in Mexico (three words) _____
20. Old draft organization (three words) _____

3. BB'S

Each answer is a two-syllable word or name in which each syllable starts with the letter B.

Ex. Spine: *Backbone*

1. Goof _____
2. British policeman _____
3. Popular doll _____
4. Lightweight furniture material _____
5. Major commercial city of India (old spelling)

   _____
6. Kind of belt _____
7. Large monkey _____
8. Sewing machine attachment _____
9. Sinclair Lewis novel _____
10. Clip joint operator? _____
11. Criticism _____
12. Chocolate treat _____
13. Weightlifter's weight _____
14. Alcoholic drink . . . or a French royal house

    _____
15. Hotel employee _____
16. Kind of chair _____
17. How Lady Godiva rode _____
18. Famous pirate _____
19. Black and yellow insect (three syllables) _____
20. Kind of account (three syllables, hyphenated)

    _____

4. BIG TEASE

Each answer is a familiar two-word phrase with the initials T. T.

Ex. Rotate in playing a game: *Take turns*

1. Contents of a David Letterman list _____
2. Vehicle that takes cars to a car pound _____
3. It has to be upright for a passenger before an airplane landing _____
4. Lively dance _____
5. Maximum span a U.S. president can be president _____
6. Ping-pong _____
7. Informal shirt that bares the shoulders _____
8. Usually the leading song on an album _____
9. Kind of wrestling _____
10. Genteel article of furniture _____
11. Item that keeps a cravat from flapping _____
12. Lessons for a very young toddler _____
13. Rails _____
14. Kind of baby _____
15. Difficult phase in early childhood _____

5. WORDS TO THE Y'S

Each answer is a word or a familiar two-word phrase or name that starts and ends with Y.

Ex. It was founded by Kublai Khan: *Yüan Dynasty*

1. It's located in New Haven, Connecticut _____
2. Beatles hit that was #1 for four weeks in 1965 _____
3. On an annual basis _____
4. Fictional locale in William Faulkner novels _____
5. Coward, in slang _____
6. Naval petty officers, as a group _____
7. Sixties TV game show hosted by Tom Kennedy _____
8. It's north of British Columbia _____
9. Biographical film about George M. Cohan _____
10. Russian poet Yevtushenko _____
11. Classic advertising slogan for Virginia Slims* _____
12. Phrase used in addressing a king or queen _____
13. Choice of vote, in the Senate _____
14. Delicious _____
15. Familiar complimentary close, on a letter _____

*Answer is a six-word phrase

6. DOUBLE W

Each answer is a compound word or a familiar two-word phrase or name in which the first part ends with W and the second part starts with W.
Ex. Shrub whose shoots were once used for making barbed missiles: *Arrowwood*.

1. Disney heroine with seven dwarfs _____
2. Wingless beetle that emits a greenish light _____
3. North and South America _____
4. One who works on the side of skyscrapers _____
5. A little dense _____
6. Maximum payload of a ballistic missile _____
7. Artist of the Helga Pictures _____
8. Ship owned by Greenpeace _____
9. Dog's bark _____
10. Snore loudly while sleeping _____
11. Spouse who was never officially married (first half of this answer is hyphenated) _____
12. One who makes or repairs certain farm implements _____
13. A literary or musical genre that makes a sharp break with the past _____
14. President before Warren Harding _____

7. LL FOR YOUR BEAN

Each answer is a word or two-part phrase or name in which each part contains LL.

Ex. City in southeast Washington: *Walla Walla*

1. Legendary Swiss archer _____
2. What people answer "Here!" for _____
3. Jazz great Morton _____
4. Slang term for a coward _____
5. Olympic sport with six players on a side _____
6. Waste time _____
7. Resentment _____
8. Outside the bounds of law _____
9. Host of the old *The Price is Right, The $10,000 Pyramid,* and other game shows _____
10. Cigarette once advertised with the slogan "I'm particular" _____
11. Boring place, in '50s slang _____
12. Broadway musical (1964–65) starring Carol Channing _____
13. Fill in the blank: October 31st is _____ Eve
14. Very revealing, as an unauthorized biography _____
15. Operator-assisted telephoning (when the charges are paid by the recipient) _____
16. Grammy-winning pop group caught lip-synching their songs _____
17. Civil War battle site (1863) in Virginia _____
18. Popular political survey _____

8. BEGIN, AGAIN

Each answer is a familiar three-word phrase in which the middle word is "the" and the first and third words begin with the same letter.

Ex. Not be on target: *Miss the mark*

1. Go to bed, in slang _____
2. Antinuclear slogan in the 1960s _____
3. Words before "angels sing" in a Christmas carol _____
4. Make a lot of noise, as a party _____
5. To tramp about, as in looking for a job _____
6. Like an illegal or unfair punch _____
7. Be in charge, as a hen in a henhouse _____
8. Run a casino out of money _____
9. Change what looks like defeat into victory _____
10. Take a painful but necessary action _____
11. Finally cut off support _____
12. Prepare a midnight snack, maybe _____

9. H-HOUR

Each answer is a familiar two-word phrase or name in which each word begins with the letter H.

Ex. Farm helper: *Hired hand*

1. Women's dressy shoes _____
2. Expression of approval, as of a speech _____
3. Wish often expressed around Christmas and Hanukkah _____
4. Former country music variety TV show _____
5. Scary part of an amusement park _____
6. Star batter on a baseball team _____
7. What a construction worker wears on his head _____
8. In "Silent Night," they sing "Hallelujah" _____
9. Top dog _____
10. Sailors' exclamation when lifting an anchor _____
11. What Heloise offered in her newspaper column _____
12. Master escape artist _____
13. Elvis Presley's first hit _____
14. Supreme happiness, in slang _____
15. Popular cheer (three words) _____

10. SPECIAL K

Each answer is a two-syllable word or phrase in which each syllable ends in the letter K.

Ex. Illegal payment: *Kickback*

1. Card game also called twenty-one _____
2. Where to find recipes _____
3. Eskimo boot _____
4. Style of proceeding with the legs apart and feet pointed outwards _____
5. Something a hiker carries _____
6. Tchotchke _____
7. It helps you keep your place when reading _____
8. Kind of joke _____
9. Approval for an unlimited expenditure _____
10. Chicago suburb famous for its Frank Lloyd Wright–designed homes _____
11. Style of music pioneered by the Ramones _____
12. Absolute regularity or precision _____
13. Dangerous, as speed _____
14. Important time for college fraternities and sororities _____
15. Howard Stern, for one _____
16. Classic host of TV's *American Bandstand* _____
17. Safecracker _____
18. Research institute involved in planning or problem solving _____

11. GOING CA-CA

Each answer is a familiar two-word phrase in which both words start with CA.

Ex. Holder for a laptop computer or other portable equipment: *Carrying case*

1. Mode of transportation in San Francisco _____
2. Sweet found in a Christmas stocking _____
3. Feline with black, yellow, and white coloring

   _____
4. Slang for a theatrical audition that's open to everyone _____
5. Where NASA blasts off _____
6. Bandleader who wrote "Minnie the Moocher"

   _____
7. TV show hosted by Allen Funt _____
8. Old-fashioned place to look things up in a library

   _____
9. National park in New Mexico _____
10. Chalk or limestone, chemically _____
11. Dessert item that contains orange specks _____
12. Latin for "beware of the dog" _____
13. In bygone times, something a visitor left when a person wasn't home _____

12. SECOND STREET

Each answer is a compound word or a familiar two-word phrase in which the first part ends with ST and the second part begins with ST.

Ex. What the horses usually get off to at the Kentucky Derby: *Fast start*

1. Something scary that's told around a campfire _____

2. Place along an interstate highway _____

3. What Custer made at Little Bighorn _____

4. This might knock out a country's nuclear capability _____

5. Famous person making a special appearance on a TV series _____

6. Cuba or North Korea, for example _____

7. Macy's slogan: "World's _____"

8. Biblical movie (1965) *The* _____ *Ever Told*

9. What a wet iron bar might leave on a floor _____

10. What makes you finally lose your patience _____

11. What the wind might cause in the dry Southwest _____

12. Nickname for Delaware _____

13. Swimming event of 100- or 200-meters _____

13. PEEPING

Each answer is a familiar two-word phrase or name with the initials P. P.

Ex. Printing trial that an editor checks for errors: *Page proof*

1. Ones corresponding regularly over a long distance _____

2. It was smoked by Indians on ceremonial occasions _____

3. Longstanding personal annoyance _____

4. Garden items that are shelled _____

5. Travelers used to go here "or bust" _____

6. Expensive Monopoly property _____

7. Very flattering bit of publicity _____

8. Thick, highly seasoned soup _____

9. Person who habitually takes medicinal tablets _____

10. He rid Hamelin of rats _____

11. Villains in *Invasion of the Body Snatchers* _____

12. Highly florid writing _____

13. What opium is extracted from _____

14. A story performance by Punch and Judy, e.g. _____

15. Honor-roll student _____

16. Disposable item to eat off of at a picnic _____

17. What the "eater" ate in a 1958 Sheb Wooley song _____

14. EASY E'S

Each answer is a familiar two-word phrase in which EE appears in both halves.
Ex. Extended period of extreme cold: *Deep freeze*

1. What the moon is said to be made of _____
2. Right guaranteed by the First Amendment _____
3. Head of a hive _____
4. Equivalent of one yard _____
5. Noted thoroughfare for London newspapers _____
6. Something excellent, in 1920s slang _____
7. Initials are often carved in its bark _____
8. Active time for fraternities and sororities _____
9. Reaching mid-leg, as mud (hyph.) _____
10. America's Junior Miss, e.g. _____
11. What golfers pay to play _____
12. Shropshire or merino, e.g. _____
13. Musical group that sang the soundtrack for *Saturday Night Fever* _____
14. Dodger Hall-of-Famer known as the "Little Colonel" (3 words) _____
15. What one little pig cried all the way home (three words) _____

15. B.C.

Each answer is a compound word or a familiar two-word phrase or name in which the first part ends with B and the second part begins with C.

Ex. Stupid person, in slang: *Dumb cluck*

1. It covers the middle of an auto wheel _____
2. North American lynx; the mascot for Ohio University _____
3. Seafood dish in the shape of a patty _____
4. Meat cut from a young sheep _____
5. Skeletal part that protects the internal organs _____
6. Bout of drinks at one bar after another _____
7. Federal program that provides employment training, begun in 1964 _____
8. Part of a train with easy chairs and a buffet _____
9. Bandleader known as the "King of Hi-De-Ho" _____
10. Longtime columnist for the San Francisco Chronicle _____
11. Yemen or Iraq, for example _____
12. Amo, amas, amat, amamus, amatis, amant, e.g. _____
13. What a scientist might wear at work _____
14. NBC sportscaster who used to host the show *Later* _____

16. OOPS

Each answer is a familiar two-word phrase or name with the initials O. O.

Ex. Club newsletter: *Official organ*

1. Part of the White House where the president works
   _____

2. Popeye's sweetheart _____

3. Sixty minutes past midnight _____

4. Tree of the mulberry family sometimes cultivated for hedges
   _____

5. Do what the commander says _____

6. Code name for the Allies' D-day invasion _____

7. Old Vaudeville comedian who starred in the original *Hellzapoppin'* _____

8. Heavy metal artist who is the former lead singer of Black Sabbath _____

9. Complete the name of this resort in Maine: _____ Beach

10. Subject of drilling controversy _____

11. Jimmy Carter's birthday; start of the tenth month
    _____

12. What the President takes at the Inauguration (three words)
    _____

13. Sign often seen on pay telephones and vending machines (three words) _____

14. Independent; without anyone else's help (three words)
    _____

15. Popular skin cream (three words) _____

17. P-NUTS

Each answer is a compound word or a familiar two-word phrase or name in which the first part ends with P and the second part begins with P.

Ex. Something to jot notes on: *Scrap paper*

1. It holds up a street light _____
2. Well-known political survey _____
3. Game in which you might lose your shirt _____
4. Something you might issue on a check you just wrote _____
5. Nonbiological mother or father _____
6. Receptacle you might put under a leaky crankcase _____
7. Hard-rock group (1960s–'70s), which the Guinness Book of World Records once named the "world's loudest band" _____
8. Elude _____
9. An upper or amphetamine _____
10. It's #1 on your list of things to do _____
11. What several doctors have when they work together _____
12. Where you might get the ink to print AIRMAIL on an envelope _____
13. Part of a china setting for a course before the entrée _____
14. S.O.S or Brillo, for example _____
15. Pod vegetables that make a sharp noise when you open them _____

18. MAMA

Each answer is a familiar two-word phrase or name in which both parts begin with the letters MA.
Ex. Felt-tipped pen: *Magic Marker*

1. One who studies calculus and topology in college

   _____

2. Nickname for the N.C.A.A. basketball tournament

   _____

3. Complete this line from *The Lone Ranger*: "Who was that _____?"

4. Nickname for socialite Sidney Biddle Barrows

   _____

5. It has a picture of Alfred E. Neuman on its cover

   _____

6. Aeronautics company that built the MX missile

   _____

7. Dustin Hoffman thriller in 1976 _____

8. Kind of paperback _____

9. Mel Gibson's first hit movie _____

10. Ex-wife of Donald Trump _____

11. Woman who anointed the feet of Jesus _____

12. Suave Italian actor who starred in *La Dolce Vita*

    _____

13. Classic figure in tobacco advertising _____

14. Rock group with the 1964 #1 hit "Do Wah Diddy Diddy"

    _____

15. Nickname for Jack Dempsey, with "the" _____

16. Robin Hood's sweetheart _____

19. HIDDEN LEAD

Each answer is a compound word or a familiar two-word phrase that contains the consecutive letters PB.

Ex. Variety of men's hat: *Snap-brim*

1. What an old-fashioned orator stood on _____
2. Kind of whale _____
3. Portable writing surface _____
4. Place to save newspaper clippings _____
5. Part of the leg that swivels _____
6. One who serves wine to the gods _____
7. Industry in Norfolk, Virginia _____
8. Result of a tie-up in a game of hoops _____
9. Chapstick, for example _____
10. Heinz container _____
11. Items sold by Dutch florists _____
12. Leftover part of a ham or roast that might be boiled _____
13. Finely powdered soot used as a pigment in paint _____
14. Head honcho _____

20. 2-D

Each answer is a familiar two-word phrase or name in which the first word ends with D and the second word starts with D.

Ex. Brazen time to pull a hold-up: *Broad daylight*

1. Thousand Island or Roquefort, e.g. _____
2. Slang for someone who drives too fast _____
3. Central part of a computer _____
4. Iditarod runner _____
5. What the Red Cross might conduct after a disaster _____
6. Risky social engagement _____
7. Tennis game with a man and woman on each side _____
8. Where boys and girls live together _____
9. Intensive questioning, as by the police _____
10. The hora, for example _____
11. Elvis Presley's #1 hit for 1956 _____
12. One who's doomed _____
13. A woman who's interested in men only for their money _____
14. Nickname for Virginia _____
15. Where to buy a Taurus or Mustang _____
16. What a weather vane indicates _____
17. It has hearts, spades, diamonds, and clubs _____
18. What you're on for nourishment if you can't eat solid foods _____
19. Nightmare _____
20. Phrase of greeting or parting _____

21. AA BATTERIES

Each answer is a two-part phrase with the initials A. A.
Ex. Twentieth-century painting genre: *Abstract art*

1. Knob on the throat _____
2. Amtrak conductor's cry _____
3. Sailors' cry upon leaving dock _____
4. Policy of helping minorities in business and education _____
5. It's less than 90° _____
6. Tropical insects that march en masse _____
7. Much-watched annual broadcast for movie fans _____
8. Building blocks from which proteins are constructed _____
9. Home of the University of Michigan _____
10. Weekly magazine for Madison Avenue workers _____
11. Company with the slogan "Something special in the air" _____
12. It begins alif, ba, ta, tha . . . _____
13. Executive's righthand person _____
14. Capital of Ethiopia _____

22. DISTRICT OF COLUMBIA

Each answer is a familiar two-word phrase or name with the initials D. C.

Ex. Where federal trials are conducted: *District court*

1. What Fido wears around his neck _____
2. What a stupid student wears on his head _____
3. Liquid-Plumr, for example _____
4. Popular beverage holder from a dispenser _____
5. Working parents' need _____
6. Outdoor seat on a ship _____
7. What a battery runs on _____
8. Where to eat on a train _____
9. Act of betrayal _____
10. Person who reviews plays _____
11. Explosive device used against a submarine

   _____
12. Item for keeping track of appointments _____
13. What ambassadors belong to _____
14. What rowdy demonstrators may be arrested for

   _____
15. Dante's masterwork _____
16. S.O.S. _____
17. Head of the government's antinarcotics program

   _____
18. Set of rules on what to wear _____
19. Where to take a dirty dress _____
20. Picture-taking device that doesn't use film _____

23. EEK!

Each answer is a familiar two-word phrase or name with the initials E. E.

Ex. Sharp perception, like a bird's: *Eagle eye*

1. Something that's dyed each spring _____
2. Shocking fish _____
3. Way to leave in case of a fire _____
4. Area formerly behind the Iron Curtain _____
5. What Reagan once called the Soviet Union _____
6. Using minimal power, as in modern appliances (hyph.) _____
7. Where to get a visa to see the Great Pyramids _____
8. The S.A.T., for example _____
9. How Madrileños speak _____
10. Houseplants whose leaves resemble parts of a pachyderm _____
11. P.M. issue of a newspaper _____
12. Teaching of grades K-6 _____
13. Charles Lamb or Alexander Pope, e.g. _____
14. Son of Martin Sheen who co-starred in *St. Elmo's Fire* _____
15. Expert in the field of machine wiring and supplying of power _____
16. Old-style newsboy's cry _____

24. ING-GOTS

Each answer is a familiar two-word phrase or name in which the first part ends in ING and the second part begins with G.

Ex. Where high-speed cars are tested: *Proving ground*

1. What pugilists wear on their hands _____
2. What a bride wears _____
3. Wrigley's product _____
4. A, B, C, or D—but not F _____
5. City in Ohio, or its university _____
6. Releasing _____
7. Carnival attraction with rifles and targets _____
8. Person who directs traffic near schools _____
9. Where a horse race begins _____
10. Nitrous oxide _____
11. Gender-bender film of 1992 starring Stephen Rea, with *The* _____
12. Song title preceding the lyric "How sweet the sound that saved a wretch like me" _____
13. Mirror _____
14. Joke that's repeated again and again during a show _____
15. Parts of a plane that are activated when nearing an airport _____

25. PH FACTOR

Each answer is a familiar two-word phrase or name with the initials P. H.

Ex. Place to play eight-ball: *Pool hall*

1. Something made of straw to wear on the head
   _____

2. Headgear for a safari _____

3. Work animal in a farmer's field _____

4. A substitute in the batting lineup _____

5. Full house or royal flush, e.g. _____

6. He said "Give me liberty or give me death"
   _____

7. It was bombed on December 7, 1941 _____

8. Military decoration _____

9. Apartment buildings owned by the government
   _____

10. New York City landmark, locale of Kay Thompson's Eloise books _____

11. Rock group with the 1967 hit "A Whiter Shade of Pale" _____

12. Comedy in 1985 about a Mafia family, for which Anjelica Houston won an Oscar _____

13. Doubleday or Knopf _____

14. Rival of Domino's _____

26. PJ'S

Each answer is a familiar two-word phrase or name with the initials P. J.

Ex. Purple-colored preserves: *Plum jelly*

1. Ordinary-looking girl _____
2. Container for gherkins _____
3. Whoopee cushion or exploding cigar _____
4. Name of more than twenty pontiffs, most recently in the 1960s _____
5. Instance of someone getting what he deserves _____
6. Seattle-based rock group led by Eddie Vedder _____
7. Beverage that helps improve your regularity _____
8. Sailor's coat _____
9. A refinish on a car _____
10. Rodgers and Hart 1940 musical starring Gene Kelly _____
11. Sitcom of the 1960s set in Hooterville _____
12. Informally, a place to get a pepperoni or a sausage and mushroom _____
13. Small, light plane that makes many short hops _____
14. Vaseline, generically _____

27. HOT SPOT

Each answer is a familiar two-word phrase or name with the initials H. S

Ex. Noted radio shock jock: *Howard Stern*

1. Someone who gets As in school _____
2. Place to get a perm _____
3. Where to buy hammers, nails, etc. _____
4. Social elite _____
5. TV game show based on tic-tac-toe _____
6. Deli item made with rye bread, maybe _____
7. What a luau dancer wears _____
8. Nickname for Indiana _____
9. Event for an equestrian _____
10. It gets added on food and makes the mouth burn _____
11. Piece of equipment for a Boston Bruin or Calgary Flame _____
12. Faster's protest _____
13. Initial advantage in a race _____
14. Part of a race just before the finish line _____

28. CB TALK

Each answer is a familiar two-word phrase or name with the initials C. B.

Ex. Snickers or 3 Musketeers, e.g.: *Candy bar*

1. What a seer gazes into _____
2. Thief who climbs in upstairs windows _____
3. Unconditional permission _____
4. Soft drink containers often compared to thick glasses _____
5. Game for Charles Goren _____
6. Short rest from office work _____
7. Young male attendant on a ship _____
8. *Superman* or *Archie*, e.g. _____
9. Distinguished chef _____
10. What a chef slices food on _____
11. Irish dish often served with cabbage _____
12. Common ingredient in suntan lotion _____
13. Longtime quiz program sponsored by G.E. _____
14. Inability to perceive different hues _____
15. Things your mother wears, in a classic putdown _____
16. Firm that rates your ability to pay debts _____
17. Area just behind home plate _____
18. Coffee and rolls, say, in the morning _____

29. LIPLOCK

Each answer is a compound or hyphenated word in which each half starts with L.

Ex. Rope that you throw to a person who's drowning: *Lifeline*

1. Kind of binder, for notebook paper _____
2. Insect known as "daddy" _____
3. People with romance problems _____
4. Like Bolivia, Switzerland, or Nepal _____
5. Flavor of Sprite _____
6. Cowardly _____
7. Dull or without flair _____
8. Person who is paid rent _____
9. Epithet for undesirable people _____
10. Kind of pine often used by woodworkers

   _____
11. _____ Plan, with which the U.S. helped its allies in World War II
12. Host Art of 1950s–'60s afternoon TV _____
13. Center of public attention or notoriety _____
14. Person who doesn't know much about sailing

   _____

30. POSTSCRIPT

Each answer is a compound word with the consecutive letters PS.

Ex. Attire for a parachutist: *Jumpsuit*

1. Something you check your oil with _____
2. Children's game played on a sidewalk _____
3. Insignificant person _____
4. Logger's tool _____
5. Woodpecker _____
6. Something that might be put on a tennis ball _____
7. Where to pitch a tent _____
8. Item in a woman's purse _____
9. Slang for "to throw away" (hyph.) _____
10. Three Stooges humor _____
11. Implement for eating a Campbell's product _____
12. Boy who is related by marriage _____
13. Tightwad _____
14. Diploma _____
15. Publisher's Clearinghouse contest _____

31. "A" THERE

Each answer is a familiar two-word phrase in which each word has a long A sound.

Ex. To cause a disturbance: *Raise Cain*

1. It's hard to keep this while telling a silly joke

   _____

2. It carries heavy goods by rail _____
3. It officially began with the launch of Sputnik

   _____

4. Backup time for a postponed game _____
5. Large, shorthaired dog _____
6. Flexible armor _____
7. Kleenex or Coca-Cola, e.g. _____
8. Common money-raising event for a church or school group _____
9. Opposite of a dieting effect _____
10. Length of time for "a week" in a Beatles hit

    _____

11. Slow rate of moving _____
12. Electrical impulses given off inside the head

    _____

13. The second largest body of water in Canada (3 words, each containing a long A sound)

    _____

32. THE LAST SHALL BE FIRST

Each answer is a familiar two-word phrase in which each word has four letters, and the last letter of the first word is the same as the first letter of the second word.
Ex. Unusual person or thing: *Rara avis*

1. Body of water that Buffalo is on _____
2. Cause for a motorist's breakdown _____
3. Free-throw shots are made behind this _____
4. Where to see races in the butterfly and backstroke

   _____
5. When traffic is most congested _____
6. Maneuver at an intersection that requires a signal

   _____
7. Charlotte Brontë heroine _____
8. Senior citizens might pay this to ride a bus

   _____
9. When a horse race begins _____
10. Hill on a beach _____
11. Lab container made of glass _____
12. Cocaine or heroin _____
13. Person who's beyond help or hope _____
14. Symbol between numbers to indicate addition

    _____
15. A long-lost friend would be a sight for these

    _____

33. THAT'S SOMETHING

Each answer is a familiar two-word phrase in which the first word starts with S and the second word starts with TH.
Ex. Illness that makes it hard to talk: *Strep throat*

1. Something odd sticks out like this _____
2. Reason to reconsider _____
3. Short, unspecified distance _____
4. Cry before "You're out!" _____
5. What a person with a lisp might seek _____
6. Branch of mathematics involving groups of things _____
7. South Carolina senator who was the oldest serving senator in U.S. history _____
8. Seasonal plays in resort communities _____
9. Weather phenomenon of March or April _____
10. It's used to stitch up a wound _____
11. One week after August 27th _____
12. Fifty times one hundred and twenty _____
13. Furtive burglar _____
14. Hallucinating _____

34. EAST SIDE

Each answer is a familiar two-word phrase or name in which the first word begins with E and the second word ends with E.
Ex. When water flows out from the shore: *Ebb tide*

1. Spring event at which people traditionally wear bonnets _____

2. What surrounds a yolk _____

3. What you have to pay to compete in a contest _____

4. Strenuous physical exertion, as scrubbing _____

5. Nickname for Ireland _____

6. Nickname for New York _____

7. It carries steam or gases away from a motor _____

8. Two U.S. dollars for one British pound, e.g. _____

9. Wisconsin city whose name is French for "clear water" _____

10. You might pull this to bring a train to a screeching halt _____

11. Cry in fencing _____

12. Provision that allows you to get out of a contract _____

13. Brand name for a chocolate-covered ice cream bar _____

14. A president might invoke it to keep secrets _____

15. It grows seed cones _____

16. Part of a football field in which to score a touchdown _____

35. ON THE DL

Each answer is a familiar two-word phrase or name with the initials D. L.

Ex. What a spy leads: *Double life*

1. Pro football team from the Motor City _____
2. Religious leader from Tibet _____
3. Spiderlike arachnid also called a harvestman _____
4. Latin or Aramaic _____
5. What college kids with good grades are on _____
6. What you might shoot somebody you don't like _____
7. You might sign a contract on this _____
8. What you get at the motor vehicle bureau _____
9. Embarrassing stuff you wouldn't want to hang out on the clothesline _____
10. Sharp turn on a golf course _____
11. What is given at an Arthur Murray Studio _____
12. Complete the famous quote: "_____, I presume"
13. Play by Mae West or its lead character _____
14. Gucci or Donna Karan _____
15. Someone you might hire to end a marriage _____

36. THE WB

Each answer is a familiar two-word phrase or name with the initials W. B.
Ex. Film studio that distributed *Casablanca: Warner Brothers*

1. Container for Chablis or Chianti _____
2. In old ads, product that helped build strong bodies _____
3. Popular encyclopedia _____
4. What a mammal has that a reptile doesn't _____
5. Someone who dampens others' enthusiasm _____
6. Place to grow flowers next to a sill _____
7. Things you manipulate in your hand to relieve stress _____
8. Flamingo or ibis _____
9. Famous place to surf in Honolulu _____
10. Another name for Aquarius _____
11. Hit from 1965 for Sam the Sham and the Pharaohs _____
12. Woman who marries just before her husband goes off to fight _____
13. February 22 _____
14. Group that forecasts precipitation and temperature _____
15. Internet Explorer, Firefox, or Safari, for example _____
16. Nickname for frontiersman Hickok _____
17. Hollow plastic sphere with holes that's hit with a bat _____
18. Locale of Bethlehem and Jericho _____
19. Things that ring in June _____
20. Greeting to a person who's been away a long time _____

37. ARMS CACHE

Each answer is a familiar two-word phrase or name in which the first word ends in AR and the second word starts with M.

Ex. Garage workers: *Car mechanic*

1. Rite of passage for a Jewish boy _____
2. Sell-off on Wall Street _____
3. Man's facial hair that curls up at the ends _____
4. Vehicle that lands on the moon _____
5. Close call _____
6. Rhythm and blues, rock and roll, or rap (but not classical) _____
7. Tree whose sap is used to make pancake syrup _____
8. Company that produces havanas _____
9. Something you wear in the winter to keep the sides of your head warm _____
10. Monument that honors fallen soldiers _____
11. Big manufacturer of cold cuts _____
12. Selection of dishes at a restaurant costing exactly 100 cents _____
13. Meter or rod, for example _____
14. Chart showing constellations _____
15. Radioactive stuff from a reactor _____
16. Exclamation meaning "Alas!" _____

38. AT THE HEART OF THE MATTER

Each answer is a compound word or a familiar two-word phrase or name in which each half has four letters and the middle two letters of the first word are the same as the middle two letters of the second.

Ex. Departed years ago: *Long gone*

1. Picnic competition that involves hopping _____
2. It has 366 days _____
3. Fenced-in area for cows, horses, or chickens

   _____

4. Absolute tie _____
5. Each one has a fairway and a green _____
6. Tennis stroke that puts backspin on the ball _____
7. Shoal _____
8. Principal canvas on a ship _____
9. Co-author of *The Communist Manifesto* _____
10. Written series of things one would love to get

    _____

11. Event for unloading unwanted summer merchandise

    _____

12. Middle ground between black and white extremes (British spelling) _____
13. Classic Pontiac muscle car; or, a Stravinsky ballet, with *The* _____
14. How much a ship can carry _____
15. Place to use a cue stick _____

39. ROW YOUR BOAT

Each answer is a familiar two-word phrase or name in which each word's second and third letters are RO.
Ex. Farmers with corn, wheat, etc.: *Crop growers*

1. Big seller of fine men's suits _____
2. Metal for a balcony railing, for example _____
3. An oath that's not followed _____
4. Place where extremely high-speed vehicles are tested, as the Bonneville Salt Flats _____
5. Traveled here and there by car _____
6. Agreement whereby two companies advertise each other's products _____
7. Fish from a babbling stream _____
8. Local unit of young Girl Scouts _____
9. Wearing-away of soil, as from a stream's bank _____
10. Money earned by a business before taxes _____
11. Refute _____
12. Old military award in Germany _____
13. Old-fashioned cable car in one of New York City's boroughs _____
14. Slangy order to remove one's pants _____

40. LEFT AND RIGHT

Each answer is a familiar two-word phrase or name in which the first word starts with L and the second word starts with R.

Ex. Popular passenger vehicle from Britain: *Land Rover*

1. Capital of Arkansas _____
2. Inflatable item on a ship _____
3. Item on top of a house that's useful during a storm _____
4. Person who knows what you're saying not by hearing _____
5. "Good Golly Miss Molly!" singer _____
6. Singer with the 1977 hit "Blue Bayou" _____
7. Singer with the #1 hits "Truly" and "Say You Say Me" _____
8. Country singer with the #1 hit "Something's Gotta Give" _____
9. Pink _____
10. Gin or vodka cocktail with fruit juice _____
11. Starring part in a movie or play _____
12. Publication for students during legal studies _____
13. Animal that runs a maze _____
14. Apparatus on top of a car _____
15. Part of a gym adjoining the showers _____
16. What you turn to when all other efforts have failed _____

41. END TO END

Each answer is a familiar two-word phrase or name in which the last two letters of the first word are the same as the first two letters of the second.
Ex. The final one of a long series of irritations: *Last straw*

1. Organization for young baseball players
   _____

2. The United States has a large one with Japan
   _____

3. Something scary that's told around a campfire
   _____

4. Symbol on Canada's flag _____
5. Common logic _____
6. Headquarters in Houston or Cape Canaveral
   _____

7. Line that runs through Greenwich, England
   _____

8. If your bank makes a mistake on your bank account, what they'd probably blame it on _____
9. Race madly about on errands _____
10. *Murder, She Wrote* star _____
11. Third largest city in Texas _____
12. Place along a highway to pull over and stretch your legs _____
13. Breed of canine that's always referred to as "old"
    _____

42. WORD PLAY

Each answer is a familiar two-word phrase or name with the initials W. P.

Ex. Something that comes up on the Internet: *Web page*

1. Home of the U.S. Military Academy _____
2. Summer toy that squirts _____
3. It might offer a reward for someone dead or alive _____
4. Former group of countries opposing NATO _____
5. Point formed in the hairline in the middle of the forehead _____
6. Sign on a bench you shouldn't sit on _____
7. Wrapping material that's not good to write on _____
8. Electrical outlet on the side of a room _____
9. Group of wild canines _____
10. Jumble or double-crostic _____
11. Professional who helps couples with their nuptials _____
12. Czar's home in old St. Petersburg _____
13. Possible requirement before buying a gun _____
14. Spot for a public flogging _____
15. Energy derived from whirling propellers _____
16. First appearance of a movie or other entertainment _____

43. FOR PROS

Each answer is a familiar two-word phrase or name in which the first word starts with P and the second word starts with RO.
Ex. Moving piece in an auto engine: *Piston rod*

1. Where the Pilgrims landed _____

2. Small women's lavatory for applying makeup, say _____

3. Business that a child with a bike might have _____

4. Big piece of beef cooked in one piece and served in its juice _____

5. Top of a house that's not at a steep angle _____

6. Colorful flower name in a Woody Allen title _____

7. Implement for applying a swath of color to a wall _____

8. Paper with holes in a self-playing keyboard instrument _____

9. Former capital of Jamaica _____

10. Fan of the Ramones, say _____

11. Way for cars that's not open to the public _____

12. Order of players on the mound in baseball _____

13. Leader of the United States during the 1930s–'40s _____

14. Televangelist who once ran for president _____

15. Actor who starred in Broadway's *Show Boat* and *The Emperor Jones* _____

16. Onetime Cincinnati Reds star _____

44. LET'S GO!

Each answer is a familiar two-word phrase or name with the initials L. G.

Ex. Things to wear on your hands when you do cleaning: *Latex gloves*

1. A truck uses it when going up a hill _____
2. Important person on a beach _____
3. Woman's makeup item _____
4. California city whose name means "the cats" _____
5. Slang term for money _____
6. In legend, she rode naked through Coventry _____
7. Body of water on the west end of Switzerland _____
8. It's deployed when a plane nears an airport _____
9. Nitrous oxide _____
10. Mirror _____
11. Someone responsible for a child in place of a parent _____
12. What a mayor or town supervisor is head of _____
13. Second in command in a state _____
14. Tract in the West once given by Congress for a college or railroad _____
15. What John Lennon played in the Beatles _____
16. It used to be dispensed from pumps into cars _____
17. Weapon that's dangerous to keep around the house _____
18. Eros or Cupid _____

46. GOOD THINKING!

Each answer is a familiar two-word phrase or name in which the first word begins with G and the second word ends with G.

Ex. Common greeting: *Good morning*

1. Animal that's a subject of experiments _____
2. Zero, in slang _____
3. Result of greenhouse gases _____
4. Possible result of an oil shortage _____
5. It flies over public buildings in Athens _____
6. Old-fashioned way of making bottles _____
7. Service that stores often provide around Christmas _____
8. Miscellany _____
9. Where a road meets a railroad track _____
10. Command to a little dogie _____
11. Edgar Allan Poe story, with *The* _____
12. Something a stripper wears _____
13. It helps a blind person get around _____
14. Sign on a business that's closed for vacation _____

45. M&MS

Each answer is a familiar two-word phrase or name in which the first word ends with M and the second word begins with M.

Ex. Cause of a computer breakdown: *System malfunction*

1. Head of a marching band _____
2. Relative of 2% in the dairy case _____
3. Occasion to do the butterfly _____
4. Star Wars episode of 1999, with *The* _____
5. Civil rights protest of the 1960's _____
6. Leader of the Doors _____
7. Old movie cowboy with the horse Tony _____
8. *Cheers* bartender _____
9. In the bestseller's title, words after *Men Are* _____ . . .
10. Branch of physics dealing with atoms and subatomic particles or waves _____
11. Chemical compound with the symbol Na_2O _____
12. Tractor and thresher, for example _____
13. Goat for Navy, or Tiger for Princeton _____
14. Popular brand of shoes _____
15. President at the turn of the twentieth century _____

47. ALL ABOUT ME

Each answer is a familiar two-word phrase or name with the initials M. E.

Ex. Slender tropical fish: *Moray eel*

1. World's tallest peak _____
2. Where Israel and Lebanon are _____
3. TV's talking horse _____
4. Person who performs autopsies _____
5. Popular NPR program _____
6. Person who runs a magazine _____
7. Expert on motors _____
8. World's Fair of 1967 _____
9. Something to mail documents in _____
10. What follows the preliminary contests _____
11. Conflicted feelings _____
12. Brad Davis film that was a 1978 Best Picture nominee _____
13. Our language as it's been spoken since about 1475 _____
14. Exclamation of disbelief _____
15. Brainwork _____

48. PLAYING LP'S

Each answer is a familiar two-word phrase or name with the initials L. P.
Ex. Trap for catching shellfish: *Lobster pot*

1. Identification on the back of a car _____
2. A bullfrog sits on it _____
3. Site of the 1980 Winter Olympics, in upstate New York _____
4. Teacher of contracts or torts _____
5. Tony Blair led it _____
6. Nadir _____
7. Safety item on a ship _____
8. What a teacher prepares for each class _____
9. American coin since 1909 _____
10. It's recited in church _____
11. Blastoff site for a rocket _____
12. White-Out _____
13. Book by Antoine de St. Exupéry, with *The* _____
14. Aphrodisiac drink _____
15. Computer product made by Hewlett-Packard _____
16. What women experience during childbirth _____
17. Cost of an item as published in a catalogue _____
18. Where a booby prize winner finishes _____

49. CONCEALED LEGS

Each answer is a familiar two-word phrase or name in which the first word ends in LE and the second word begins with G.
Ex. Automobile lubricant: *Axle grease*

1. Something you chew and blow _____
2. Kind of bread, made with unprocessed ingredients _____
3. Where a war is fought _____
4. Item of playground equipment _____
5. Stoves, washers, and big machines, from an economist's standpoint _____
6. Bill Clinton or George Bush, scholastically speaking _____
7. Device that shoots metal fasteners _____
8. Jim Carrey comedy of 1996, with *The* _____
9. She played Bea Arthur's mother on *The Golden Girls* _____
10. Garden product brand _____
11. Dingy and off-white—like clothes that aren't washed well _____
12. Chess, monopoly, or ping-pong _____
13. Load on a large truck, which has a danger of exploding _____
14. Lag in military production between two countries _____
15. Chitter-chatter _____
16. What a turkey says _____

50. SIX-POINTERS

Each answer is a familiar two-word phrase or name with the initials T. D.

Ex. It helps you tear off a piece of adhesive: *Tape dispenser*

1. Activity in which you click your heels _____
2. What an auto dealer invites you to take in a new car _____
3. The inability to distinguish pitch in musical sounds _____
4. Reason for a filling _____
5. Thick book that may include the Yellow Pages _____
6. What shook the world, in a classic book by John Reed _____
7. A charitable contribution or state taxes, on an IRS form _____
8. Martin Scorsese film of 1976 _____
9. What a TV station tells you it's experiencing when a program stops suddenly _____
10. Cubed candy made with fruit juice and dusted with sugar _____
11. In China it lasted from A.D. 618 to 907 _____
12. Leader, slangily _____
13. A doctor uses it when you say "Ahhhh" _____
14. Günter Grass novel, with *The* _____
15. Small marsupial from Down Under _____
16. Harding administration scandal _____

51. NEW AT HEART

Each answer is a familiar two-word phrase in which the first word ends with NE and the second word starts with W. Ex. Representation of periodic oscillations, in physics: *Sine wave*

1. Street sign with an arrow _____
2. Common property barrier in New England _____
3. Riesling or Müller-Thurgau, e.g. _____
4. Famous old stock brokerage _____
5. Man who prefers to live or work by himself _____
6. To clean clothes not by hand (hyph.) _____
7. Actress who won an Oscar for *The Three Faces of Eve* _____
8. Noted African-American congresswoman from CA _____
9. Female doctor in the Old West _____
10. Women use them to captivate men _____
11. What oil helps reduce in a car _____
12. Ones who dig for ore or diamonds _____
13. It hangs from pole to pole along the street _____
14. Over and _____ (finished)

52. LOS ANGELES

Each answer is a familiar two-word phrase or name with the initials L. A.

Ex. Kind of award for a body of work: *Lifetime achievement*

1. College subjects like history, English, biology, etc. _____

2. Area south of the United States _____

3. Twenty-one, for drinking _____

4. Numbing of part of the body _____

5. Holdings that are easily convertible to money _____

6. Four o'clock or 5:00 P.M. _____

7. What a southpaw pitcher throws with _____

8. Place to fly into New York _____

9. Satchmo _____

10. Kareem Abdul-Jabbar, originally _____

11. Smaller guns, but not cannon _____

12. Old-fashioned term for a tomato _____

13. Terrier from Tibet _____

14. Author/publisher go-between _____

15. Years back _____

53. TUTEES

Each answer is a familiar two-word phrase or name in which each word has two T's (not necessarily consecutively) Ex. Bit of sewing around a hole in a shirt: *Buttonhole stitch*

1. Competition between Coke and Pepsi, say _____
2. What a party loyalist votes _____
3. Informal nickname for Alabama _____
4. Stationary person or thing wide-open to attack _____
5. Item left in an ashtray _____
6. Prosecuting officer for local government _____
7. It builds up in clothes in the dryer _____
8. An aide for a high school teacher _____
9. Idea or bit of philosophizing _____
10. Modern crime involving credit cards _____
11. Cat box filler _____
12. Part of Canada above Alberta and Saskatchewan _____
13. Plays or other entertainments performed outdoors in the city _____
14. Image that used to be on TV during the wee hours of the morning _____
15. Federal agency administered by Condoleezza Rice or Colin Powell _____

54. SPLIT ENDS

Each answer is a familiar two-word phrase or name in which the first word ends in EN and the second word begins with D.

Ex. Carpenter's pin: *Wooden dowel*

1. One week _____
2. Invitation to enter a room _____
3. What you do to the hatches _____
4. Rum cocktail served with finely crushed ice _____
5. Variety of apple _____
6. Overtime period in which the first team to score wins
   _____
7. Whom Abraham Lincoln debated in 1858 _____
8. Sharp-penned op-ed columnist for the New York Times
   _____
9. Frankfurter made with the meat of a fowl _____
10. Jewish star _____
11. Widow of a king _____
12. Prime minister's street address in London _____
13. Where a can-opener and eating utensils are kept
    _____
14. Pulitzer-winning author of *Advise and Consent*, 1959
    _____
15. Comedienne who came out on her sitcom _____
16. Rock group with the chart-topping album *Dookie*
    _____
17. Brand of ice cream (hyph.) _____

55. POSTSCRIPT II

Each answer is a familiar two-word phrase or name in which the first word ends in P and the second word starts with S.
Ex. Hush-hush: *Top secret*

1. Something octagonal on a street corner _____
2. Chinese dish that isn't really Chinese _____
3. Lather from washing _____
4. The lesser-played half of a record _____
5. One-piece garment for women _____
6. Amount of money paid all at once _____
7. Private educational institution before college _____
8. A tiny amount of time added to the world's clocks about once a year _____
9. In *Star Trek,* a velocity faster than light _____
10. Areas of the universe far from earth _____
11. Capsule in which John Glenn circled the Earth in 1962 _____
12. Informal group discussion _____
13. Police action that requires a person to remove his or her clothes _____
14. Basic spiel from a politician on the campaign trail _____
15. Dress that has an apparatus underneath to flare it out _____
16. Seafood dish grilled or sautéed in butter and garlic _____

56. OVERTIME

Each answer is a familiar two-word phrase or name with the initials O. T.

Ex. Early Ron Howard TV role: *Opie Taylor*

1. First half of the Bible _____
2. Ship from the Mideast _____
3. Symbol of sturdiness _____
4. Path for pioneers in the Old West _____
5. If you have a bad heart or kidney, what you might get _____
6. What a patient lies on for surgery _____
7. It might go over your bed to help you breathe _____
8. Thornton Wilder play _____
9. Dickens hero _____
10. It's lit for quadrennial games _____
11. Face-to-face exam _____
12. Toll road between Indiana and Pennsylvania _____
13. Traditionally, the day Columbus discovered America _____
14. Tall structure that sightseers look out of _____
15. Newspaper published across the bay from San Francisco _____
16. It's usually about 400 degrees for baking chicken _____

57. MASTER OF CEREMONY

Each answer is a familiar two-word phrase or name in which the first word ends in M and the second word begins wih C.

Ex. Transportation in New York's Central Park: *Hansom cab*

1. It may wake you up in the morning _____
2. It's produced by an atomic blast _____
3. A slightly sweet thin biscuit made of whole wheat flour

   _____

4. Tiny room where you keep mops and other cleaning implements _____
5. Something spread on a bagel _____
6. It sucks up dirt _____
7. Planner of an art exhibit for a cultural institution _____
8. It may be labeled "New England" or "Manhattan"

   _____

9. Period in school for physical education _____
10. Gin drink with lemon, sugar, and selzer _____
11. Chemical name for table salt _____
12. Excerpt shown on a movie review show _____
13. Controversial topic of medical research _____
14. Where you might take refuge during a tornado _____
15. What you might change into after getting cold and wet

    _____

16. Star of *Liar Liar* and *The Truman Show* _____
17. Real name for Buffalo Bill _____
18. Percussion part of a marching band _____

58. SUPERSONIC

Each answer is a familiar two-word phrase or name in which the first word ends in SS and the second word starts with T.

Ex. Evergreen with scalelike leaves: *Cypress tree*

1. Event for Gary Kasparov _____
2. First lady of the 1940s and '50s _____
3. You can talk on this as you walk around _____
4. Beauty queen from Houston or Dallas _____
5. Opposite of a local _____
6. When you're serious about something, you get down to these _____
7. Excursion for a school group _____
8. Someone who works to improve your physical condition _____
9. A doctor might administer one to check on your heart _____
10. Nineteenth-century New York City political honcho _____
11. Buses, trains, subways, etc. _____
12. Instrument with a slide that has a low sound _____
13. Airline passenger who might rack up frequent flier miles _____
14. Dick Tracy's love _____
15. Something you're told not to remove from a product except under penalty of law _____

59. THE SHORT AND THE LONG OF IT

Each answer is a compound word or a familiar two-word phrase or name in which the first part has a short A vowel sound and the second part has a long A sound.

Ex. Cover for a light: *Lampshade*

1. Seafood dish that Baltimore is famous for _____
2. Cookout on a beach _____
3. Nike or Coca-Cola _____
4. Nine-to-five grind _____
5. Two shakes of a _____
6. If you crawl around on the lawn, you might get this on your knee _____
7. Housing in a car engine _____
8. Slang term for the fashion business _____
9. Where Broadway actors wait before performing _____
10. Letters that famous actors get _____
11. Action when you meet someone or close a deal _____
12. Painful problem at the end of your finger _____
13. Vice president under the first President Bush _____
14. Slab of meat that comes from the rear of a hog _____
15. Large pipe carrying methane, e.g. _____
16. They accompany raisins in breakfast cereal _____
17. Betting activity with a pair of dice _____
18. Kind of course in which students don't get grades A, B, C, and D _____
19. Kitsch _____
20. When basketball players run down the court quickly

    _____

60. STP

Each answer is a familiar two-word phrase or name in which the first word ends in ST and the second word starts with P.
Ex. Meat dish popular in Chinese restaurants: *Roast pork*

1. The pronoun "I," grammatically speaking _____
2. Award for *Braveheart* or *Titanic* _____
3. What you pay if you pay the full amount for something _____
4. Image on a TV screen after a station has gone off the air _____
5. Where future army officers go to college _____
6. Conduit for engine fumes _____
7. Where to keep a watch that's on a chain _____
8. The word "sung" in the trio "sing, sang, sung" _____
9. Time off during kindergarten _____
10. What an umpire wears in baseball _____
11. Complete the opening line from "Evangeline": "This is the _____"
12. Prostitution, according to a phrase _____
13. What early explorers of the New World tried to find _____
14. What Nikolai Lenin headed in Russia _____
15. Where table scraps and such go in the backyard _____
16. What a booby prize is for _____

61. INSIDE THE O.R.

Each answer is a familiar two-word phrase or name in which the first word ends in O and the second word starts with R.

Ex. Classic Campbell's soup: *Tomato rice*

1. Where San Juan is _____
2. Floor covering made by Southwest Indians _____
3. Amount of space for carrying things, as on a ship _____
4. Author of *The Joys of Yiddish* _____
5. Noted Mexican muralist _____
6. Erskine Caldwell novel made into a movie and a Broadway play _____
7. James Bond spoof from 1967 _____
8. It forms Kentucky's northern border _____
9. Transaction at Blockbuster _____
10. Guest appearance _____
11. Famous broadcaster of Japanese propaganda in World War II _____
12. It has perforations that make music when pegs are passed through them _____
13. Person who improves old snapshots _____
14. King's highway, in Spanish _____
15. How money is distributed so everyone gets an equal share _____
16. Cry at a Washington football game _____

62. REGISTERED NURSE

Each answer is a familiar two-word phrase or name with the initials R. N.

Ex. What a nasty comment might strike: *Raw nerve*

1. Not a pseudonym _____
2. X for 10, or C for 100 _____
3. Its ships fly the Union Jack _____
4. This very instant _____
5. What Barry Goldwater won in 1964 and Bob Dole won in 1996 _____
6. Perennial anticorporate presidential candidate

   _____
7. In the spring it holds pale blue eggs _____
8. One thousand, for example, rather than 999 or 1001 _____
9. Book genre that Barbara Cartland was famous for

   _____
10. Symptom of a cold or flu _____
11. Group of stations that broadcast together

    _____
12. Fifties and sixties heartthrob who sang "Be-Bop Baby" _____
13. First U.S. president to travel to China _____
14. Drink with Scotch and Drambuie _____
15. What kidnappers send the kidnapper's family

    _____

63. FM STATION

Each answer is a familiar two-word phrase or name with the initials F. M.

Ex. It helps relieve a stuffy nose and fever: *Flu medicine*

1. Letters to a celebrity _____
2. Fine steak _____
3. Place to buy and sell used items _____
4. Gold Medal factory _____
5. Bills, but not coins _____
6. Feature of capitalism _____
7. Something a baseball catcher wears _____
8. Early term for an airplane _____
9. Output of Pete Seeger and Woody Guthrie _____
10. Its defense inspired Francis Scott Key to write "The Star-Spangled Banner" _____
11. Mustache with long, droopy ends _____
12. When the Supreme Court convenes in October _____
13. Publicly traded, federally backed security _____
14. What a general practitioner practices _____
15. Person who oversees a building's safety code _____
16. It may provide relief for tired heels, arches, and toes _____
17. Cabinet member in other countries who oversees diplomatic relations _____
18. Stage show in which male performers show everything _____

64. A TO B

Each answer is a familiar two-word phrase or name in which the
first word ends with A and the second word starts with B.
Ex. Ingredient in suntan lotion: *Cocoa butter*

1. Vegetable named for a city in Peru _____
2. Leading dancer in a ballet company _____
3. Piece of furniture that can be converted for sleeping
   _____
4. Device that answers questions at parties _____
5. Someone who loves *Carmen* and *Aida* _____
6. Black-and-white animal from China in the Washington
   Zoo _____
7. The Northern Lights _____
8. It might help a defendant get a reduced sentence
   _____
9. It might hold a Nikon or a Kodak _____
10. California city that was once the name of a daytime soap
    opera _____
11. Home of the NFL's Buccaneers _____
12. Annual college football championship held in Tempe,
    Arizona _____
13. World Series champs in 1995 _____
14. Tiny annoyance for a dog _____
15. Musical group that plays Polish dance tunes _____
16. Competitor of the World Book _____
17. Florida city known for auto racing _____
18. It cools an ocean's shore _____

65. SEPTEMBER

Each answer is a familiar two-word phrase or name in which the first word ends in SE and the second word starts with P.

Ex. Sherwin-Williams product that's applied to the outside of a home: *House paint*

1. Identification on the front or back of a car _____
2. What seeing a ghost might give you _____
3. What friends may throw for you on your birthday _____
4. Flower part that's a common ingredient in perfume _____
5. Car honking, air horns, and other unwanted sounds _____
6. Waxy implement for writing on glossy surfaces _____
7. Head of government in Beijing _____
8. Phrase before "hot" and "cold" in a nursery rhyme _____
9. Air-filled snack food that can leave your fingers orange _____
10. Flat item beside a computer, used to help move the cursor _____
11. Lead someone down the _____
12. French scientist after whom a programming language is named _____
13. Primetime soap opera that co-starred Heather Locklear _____
14. Athlete who uses a stick to score a goal _____
15. Telling someone to do something when you want them to do the exact opposite _____

66. LOOKING U.P.

Each answer is a familiar two-word phrase or name with the initials U. P.

Ex. Person involved in city development: *Urban planner*

1. News agency: _____ International
2. Instrument smaller than a baby grand _____
3. Company that helped build the first transcontinental railway _____
4. Part of Michigan above Lake Michigan _____
5. Like a good golf score _____
6. Rightmost column in an addition column _____
7. Cruel and _____
8. Publisher of academic books _____
9. Support for telephone wires, electric cables, etc. _____
10. Insurance that covers everything _____
11. *Airport, Jaws,* and other films made by a particular studio _____
12. What a deodorant stops _____
13. Where nuclear material is processed _____
14. Hawaiian musician _____
15. Planters product with no sodium _____

67. SEE WHAT I.C.

Each answer is a familiar two-word phrase or name with the initials I. C.

Ex. Psychological problem of not knowing who one is: *Identity crisis*

1. Main ingredient of a sundae _____
2. Kind of engine _____
3. Hot drink topped with whipped cream _____
4. It used to separate Eastern and Western Europe _____
5. West African country that gained its independence in 1960 _____
6. Maize _____
7. Allstate or Aetna _____
8. Miraculous beginning for Jesus' mother, Mary _____
9. It might make you feel below everyone else _____
10. Part of the hospital where severly sick or injured cases are _____
11. Sleuth in the *Pink Panther* movies _____
12. Comedienne who appeared with Sid Caesar on *Your Show of Shows* _____
13. Mathematical invention of Leibniz _____
14. Historical novel set in ancient Rome published in 1934 _____
15. Polaroid _____
16. Item that may contain a speaker's notes in the size of 3½" × 5" _____
17. Business dealings between New York and California, for example _____

68. NET HOLDINGS

Each answer is a hyphenated word or a familiar two-word phrase or name in which the first part ends with NE and the second part starts with T.

Ex. What the Geneva Convention guarantees prisoners: *Humane treatment*

1. Kind of comb you might conduct a search with _____
2. Something with needles that often grows on a mountain _____
3. Repeatedly leaving messages on each other's answering machines _____
4. Something you might buy from Delta or Continental _____
5. Toll road that goes from the New Hampshire border to Augusta _____
6. What the ten Commandments were written on _____
7. It's between an incisor and a premolar _____
8. Person with a crystal ball _____
9. Three-sided figure with unequal sides _____
10. Item with a flame for welding _____
11. An extra amount you pay at the pump _____
12. Absolutely exhausted _____
13. Product advertised with the slogan "Where the rubber meets the road" _____
14. What a light that goes on on your dashboard might signal _____
15. Something that may be in the backyard and holds household fuel _____
16. Sacagawea belonged to this _____
17. Scary in an eerie way _____
18. A simpler way of saying eighteen-twentieths _____
19. An oenologist _____
20. What you might make to a bride and groom at a wedding reception _____

69. ESSEN

Each answer is a familiar two-word phrase or name with initials S. N.

Ex. California mountain range: *Sierra Nevada*

1. Popular Christmas carol _____
2. A captured soldier is supposed to reveal only his name, rank and _____
3. Nickname for Jenny Lind _____
4. Protection for a tightrope walker _____
5. Musical tone that's off _____
6. What sleeping in an awkward position can give you

   _____
7. Habits, characteristics, etc. that are so deeply ingrained that they're almost automatic _____
8. Swirling set of stars in outer space _____
9. Mythical creature sometimes called an oceanid

   _____
10. Harry Houdini, Red Buttons, or Eminem, for example

    _____
11. Belgian with the 1963 hit "Dominique" _____
12. Actor who starred in *Jurassic Park* _____
13. Blunt end, as of a pistol or pliers _____
14. Poisonous powder used in the manufacturing of mirrors _____
15. What a lover whispers into his darling's ear

    _____
16. Bringer of Christmas presents _____

70. O. H.?

Each answer is a familiar two-word phrase or name with the initials O. H.

Ex. Common furnace: *Oil heater*

1. Party that new homeowners might throw _____
2. Nine to five, commonly _____
3. Fifty + Fifty _____
4. *How the* _____ *Lives*
5. Stories that get passed down from generation to generation _____
6. Partner of Stan Laurel _____
7. Partner of Richard Rodgers _____
8. Longtime senator from Utah _____
9. Shout used to get someone's attention _____
10. Group of islands off the west coast of Scotland _____
11. Present, as supplies _____
12. Popular candy bar _____
13. Nickname for Andrew Jackson _____
14. Man's fancy headwear worn at La Scala _____
15. Beijing, in 2008 _____

71. HA!

Each answer is a familiar two-word phrase or name with the initials H. A.

Ex. Ulterior motive: *Hidden agenda*

1. Device that fits in the ear _____
2. Macaulay Culkin movie (1990) _____
3. Nickname for the sixteenth president _____
4. Nickname for someone who's good at odd jobs _____
5. Common term for a myocardial infarction _____
6. Person next in line to take the throne _____
7. Pompous talk, as in what a politician may be full of _____
8. Keeping someone confined to where he lives _____
9. Corrosive, fuming liquid _____
10. Popular car from Japan _____
11. One who emotes on stage _____
12. Well-known bikers' group _____
13. Rags-to-riches writer _____
14. It begins aleph, beth, gimel, etc. _____
15. Graphology _____
16. Mel Brooks spoof of Alfred Hitchcock _____

72. I.M.ING

Each answer is a familiar two-word phrase or name with the initials I. M.

Ex. Quick electronic communication: *Instant message*

1. Something usually found on every floor of a hotel _____

2. Nickname for boxer Tyson _____

3. Footwear often decorated with beads _____

4. Philippine leader famous for her shoe collection _____

5. An Irish author, she was the subject of a 2001 film _____

6. Football infraction made before the ball is snapped _____

7. Ralph Ellison novel about race relations _____

8. "_____ want to know"

9. Part of China bordering Ulaanbaatar's country _____

10. Book that comes with a computer or appliance _____

11. Alternative to butter that puts a crown on your head _____

12. Feature shown on a long airplane trip _____

13. It powers a yacht _____

14. Charge not quite as serious as murder _____

15. Latin phrase starting a tribute to the recently deceased _____

16. Last words of the Wicked Witch of the West _____

73. P.O. BOX

Each answer is a familiar two-word phrase or name with the initials P. O.

Ex. Chance to pose for the camera: *Photo op*

1. Cop _____
2. Where Hawaii is _____
3. What Bush took on Inauguration Day _____
4. Star of *Lawrence of Arabia* _____
5. Musical instrument in a church _____
6. Something you give someone to get them to stop fighting with you _____
7. What a Gallup poll measures on an issue _____
8. What Communism forbids for property _____
9. Shrub whose leaves can give you a rash _____
10. Theater musicians who play in a recessed area _____
11. Classic cereal consisting of air-filled grain _____
12. Dominance hierarchy showing status from highest to lowest _____
13. Mollusk that produces a gem _____
14. Extract from goobers, used in making margarine and soap _____
15. Front of a newspaper _____

74. A/C

Each answer is a familiar two-word phrase or name with the initials A. C.

Ex. Slatted seat designed for outdoor use: *Adirondack chair*

1. Where you go if you don't like a legal decision

   _____

2. What a businessperson carries papers in _____

3. A Brinks vehicle _____

4. What Dear Abby writes _____

5. Big military ship that has planes on its decks

   _____

6. It wakes you up in the morning _____

7. Where to learn to solve equations _____

8. Animal that prowls back streets _____

9. Friend of the court, in Latin _____

10. Kids' dessert items in the shapes of lions, elephants, etc.

    _____

11. Prefix at the start of a telephone number _____

12. Mystery writer who created Hercule Poirot _____

13. Egypt, Yemen, or Saudi Arabia, e.g. _____

14. International agreement to reduce weapons

    _____

15. Ordinary household electricity _____

16. French existentialist who won a Nobel Prize

    _____

17. Industrialist who gave money to found many libraries

    _____

18. Book on your desk with dates _____

75. ALTERNATIVES

Each answer is a familiar two-word phrase or name in which both words contain the consecutive letters OR.

Ex. Neighborhood place to buy a quart of milk: *Corner store*

1. Piece of fiction not as long as a novel _____
2. Pyongyang's country _____
3. Home of Texas Christian University _____
4. Person who gives a kidney or a heart _____
5. Twining plant with funnel-shaped flowers _____
6. Piece of paper you fill out to buy goods from a catalog _____
7. Listing in the Guinness Book _____
8. Veterinarian specializing in equine practice _____
9. Person in charge of athletic reporting in a newspaper _____
10. Author of *1984* _____
11. Tennis champion from Sweden, five-time winner of Wimbledon _____
12. Danish pianist and comedian _____
13. Largest city in the Beaver State _____
14. Mountainous region of Afghanistan _____
15. Northern lights _____
16. Rudy Giuliani, now _____
17. Verbatim (3 words, all containing OR) _____

76. KP DUTY

Each answer is a compound word in two syllables in which K ends the first part and P begins the second.
Ex. Lottery prize: *Jackpot*

1. Where the pilot sits _____
2. It's what you might put your lunch and supplies in when you go hiking _____
3. A large supply held in reserve for future need _____
4. Scarf or other item wound around the body above the shoulder _____
5. It might say "Ex libris" _____
6. Variety of bowling with small balls _____
7. Able to resist jolts, as a watch _____
8. Person who might steal your wallet _____
9. Snap-brimmed hat usually made of felt _____
10. Person with nutty ideas _____
11. Office or factory, for example _____
12. Summer resort in Massachusetts that has the same name as a brand of shoe _____
13. Another name for garbanzo beans _____
14. Station between two military zones _____

77. RH FACTOR

Each answer is a familiar two-word phrase or name with the initials R. H.

Ex. Where a western farmer lives: *Ranch house*

1. Something that's deliberately misleading _____
2. Place of convalescence for the elderly _____
3. What most people write with _____
4. One who drives in two lanes, maybe _____
5. Hero in Sherwood Forest _____
6. Child's toy with a saddle and reins _____
7. It might be used to water the lawn _____
8. Jewish high holy day _____
9. Title for a prince or princess _____
10. *The* _____ *Picture Show*
11. Amount of water vapor in the air, as expressed in weather forecasts _____
12. What a square peg has trouble fitting in __ _____
13. When traffic is most congested _____
14. Person who's done something in the fastest time, e.g. _____
15. Doris Day co-star _____
16. *My Fair Lady* actor _____
17. *Pal Joey* actress also known as the "Love Goddess" _____
18. *Apollo 13* director _____
19. School attended by Archie and Jughead _____
20. Rival of Simon and Schuster _____

78. ALL EARS

Each answer is a familiar two-word phrase or name in which the first word ends in E and the second word begins with AR.
Ex. Lineup of soldiers, tanks, etc.: *Battle array*

1. Someone who isn't allowed to leave home may be under this _____

2. Magician who can get out of handcuffs or a straitjacket _____

3. Part that holds a needle on a phonograph _____

4. Illustrations left by primitive man, for example _____

5. City neighboring Phoenix in the Grand Canyon state _____

6. Thin sheets of metal used for protection in battle _____

7. Piece written for *Time* or *The Atlantic,* for example _____

8. Library for illustrations _____

9. One showing up after the deadline _____

10. Former name of the comedienne whose maiden name was Barr _____

11. Daughter of Lucille Ball _____

12. Star of 1950s TV's *Our Miss Brooks* _____

13. Hall of Fame jockey who won the Kentucky Derby five times _____

14. Sword, pistol, or other small weapon _____

15. Military force based in Beijing _____

16. Place with lots of pinball machines _____

79. C. I. TOLD YOU SO

Each answer is a familiar two-word phrase or name with the initials C. I.

Ex. Popular salad dressing: *Creamy Italian*

1. Famous amusement park in Brooklyn _____
2. Baseball team in Ohio _____
3. Electric item that can put a wave in the hair _____
4. Offering for drivers from Allstate or Geico _____
5. One of the Big Three automakers' models 1930s–'70s _____
6. Unit of measure for newspaper classifieds _____
7. Title for Mr. Morse in the Colin Dexter mysteries _____
8. Brown covering for a cake _____
9. Whatever copy of a magazine is on newsstands _____
10. _____ Agency, for spies
11. Option on modern telephones that allows you to screen incoming messages _____
12. Something to save in the expectation that it will increase in value _____
13. Before computers, this listed all the books in a library _____
14. Money earned on a bank account in which the base includes money previously earned _____
15. Production of goods for sale from home _____
16. Cry before "_____The cops!"

80. VERY FINE

Each answer is a familiar two-word phrase or name with the initials V. F.

Ex. Cabinet for manila folders: *Vertical file*

1. It might lead to a stolen election _____
2. Where George Washington spent the winter of 1777–78 _____
3. Artificial ingredient in white ice cream _____
4. Stylish magazine that was once edited by Tina Brown _____
5. Large area of trees that's never been cut _____
6. Cooking grease that does not come from animals _____
7. Famous sight on the Zambezi River in southern Africa _____
8. Former president of Mexico _____
9. Nickname for Mel Torme _____
10. It follows the third tome in an encyclopedia _____
11. Nonprofessional who fights blazes _____
12. Plant that catches and eats insects _____
13. It flies over government buildings in Hanoi _____
14. Stringed instruments like the cello and double bass are part of it _____
15. Sonnet or limerick, for example _____
16. What Canada geese fly in _____

81. FOR VETERAN'S DAY

Each answer is a familiar two-word phrase or name in which the first word ends in VE and the second word starts with T.
Ex. Government levy that affects the wealthy the most: *Progressive tax*

1. Romantic arrangement involving three people _____

2. Rush hour period when a radio audience is at its peak _____

3. It immediately precedes Ash Wednesday _____
4. Immoral activity that went on before the Civil War _____

5. Founder of Wendy's _____
6. How often Francis Ford Coppola won Oscars _____

7. Sticky stuff that holds a bandage in place _____
8. Esophagus, stomach, and colon, to food _____
9. Exaggerated or deceptive language, in slang _____

10. Bundles of fibers that carry signals through the body _____

11. Anyone's first language _____
12. Blue eyes or red hair, genetically _____
13. Programming that's not taped _____
14. Kind of radio that Rush Limbaugh does _____
15. Popular brand of stuffing _____
16. Source of a small, green, Mediterranean fruit _____

82. BRR!

Each answer is a familiar two-word phrase or name in which the first word starts with BR and the second word starts with R.

Ex. European flower with hooked prickles: *Bramble rose*

1. Something to follow in *The Wizard of Oz* _____

2. Uncle Remus character _____

3. In a contest that has no actual prize, this is what you're said to win _____

4. Respite, or a space to rest or think _____

5. Side dish at a Chinese restaurant _____

6. Crimson or scarlet _____

7. Phrase for someone who goes on and on about the same thing _____

8. In a fancy home, where you might eat the first meal of the day _____

9. Person who fixes a car that can't be made to stop _____

10. When a woman is getting married, she may sign up for this for gifts _____

11. New York's _____ Parkway, named for a waterway in New York City's northernmost borough

12. A.L. MVP in 1964 who played for the Baltimore Orioles _____

13. Nuclear device in which more fissile material is produced than consumed _____

83. OPERATING ROOM

Each answer is a familiar two-word phrase or name with the initials O. R.

Ex. Variety of cookie: *Oatmeal raisin*

1. Tennessee city known for nuclear research _____
2. Televangelist who once founded a university _____
3. It's where you set a cake to bake _____
4. It separates Indiana and Kentucky _____
5. Device for pumping petroleum from the ground _____
6. Musical event in a church _____
7. Side order at a fast-food restaurant _____
8. Fine floor covering from Asia _____
9. Famous name in popcorn _____
10. Singer with the 1968 hit "The Dock of the Bay" _____
11. Tragedy by Sophocles _____
12. California team that lost in Super Bowl XXXVII _____
13. Field of work of the Gallup company _____
14. Russian event of 1917 _____
15. Christianity, Judaism, Islam, etc., collectively _____
16. Citrus bit used in marmalade _____
17. At a gas station: 87, 89, 91 or 93 _____
18. Alternative to "extra crispy" at KFC _____

84. INSIDE WARNER BROS

Each answer is a compound word in which W ends the first part of the word and B begins the second.
Ex. Reversion to an ancestor: *Throwback*

1. Something you paddle _____
2. Slang for a $10 bill _____
3. Prying tool _____
4. Infant that's less than a day old _____
5. Appealing to baser interests, as entertainment

   _____
6. Roy Rogers in the movies _____
7. Cowardly; also a kind of sapsucker _____
8. Modern winter sport done on hills _____
9. Endearingly eccentric _____
10. Do some training in a ring _____
11. Operating on a limited number of frequencies, in telephony _____
12. Fruit with its seeds on the outside _____
13. Hollywood and such, informally _____
14. Entrance to a castle that can be lifted up _____
15. To harangue _____
16. Piece of candy that's very difficult to bite into

    _____

85. NC-17

Each answer is a familiar two-word phrase or name with the initials N. C.

Ex. Raleigh's home: *North Carolina*

1. Event where reporters ask questions _____
2. Front of a rocket _____
3. Where the Democrats and Republicans nominate their presidential candidates _____
4. Site of judicial proceedings after dark _____
5. Place for people with no clothes on _____
6. Informal term for a CPA _____
7. French style of cooking _____
8. Plea in which a defendant does not dispute the charges _____
9. English playwright who wrote *Blithe Spirit* _____
10. Oscar-winning actor for *Leaving Las Vegas* _____
11. She had #1 R&B hits with "Miss You Like Crazy" and "I've Got Love On My Mind" _____
12. "Thou shalt not bear false witness" for Jews and most Protestants _____
13. It happened in England in 1066 _____
14. Emma Lazarus poem inscribed on the base of the Statue of Liberty (with "The") _____
15. Chocolate candy bar with rice inside _____
16. Where a boxer goes after he's knocked out his opponent _____
17. It trims the ends of your fingers and toes _____

86. LONG ISLAND

Each answer is a familiar two-word phrase or name with the initials L. I.

Ex. Foot soldiers with minimal equipment: *Light infantry*

1. Section of a city with lots of trattorias _____
2. Something you buy for the security of a spouse or family _____
3. Part of the digestive tract _____
4. Midwest city near Purdue University _____
5. Shackles _____
6. Frozen treat that's yellow _____
7. Common means of administering the death penalty _____
8. Kind of veto _____
9. Earning less than $15,000/year, say _____
10. Having a blood alcohol level of more than .08% _____
11. Former head of Chrysler _____
12. One who teaches students how to conjugate "amo" _____
13. Film character who's the object of the lead character's romantic feelings _____
14. Fancy appointment in a luxury car _____
15. Event of March 4, 1861, in Washington, D.C._____

87. FOR FATHER'S DAY

Each answer is a familiar two-word phrase or name with the initials F. D.

Ex. What is earned by gaining 10 yards in football: *First down*

1. Top of an aircraft carrier _____
2. Obsolescent item on which to store computer information _____
3. Group with the 1967 hit "Up Up and Away" _____
4. Salad topping that is made with catsup, oil, and vinegar _____
5. Where you usually greet visitors who come to your house _____
6. Rum cocktail made with crushed ice _____
7. Value of an Abraham Lincoln bill _____
8. Stephen Spielberg or Martin Scorsese _____
9. Christian Dior or Donna Karan _____
10. Wall Street and environs, to New York City _____
11. Trendy way to lose weight _____
12. Term for Harry Truman's administration _____
13. Substance sprinkled by Tinkerbell in *Peter Pan* _____
14. Doe _____
15. Where to buy a Mustang or Explorer _____
16. Podiatrist _____
17. Event in which students evacuate a school _____
18. Traditional Fourth of July event _____

88. INTERESTING

Each answer is a familiar two-word phrase or name in which the first word ends in IN and the second word begins with T.

Ex. Place to grab discount items at a sale: *Bargain table*

1. What a railroad runs on _____
2. Group of very smart advisers _____
3. Very sharp change of direction, as on a mountain road _____
4. What Denver residents set their clocks on

   _____
5. Decathlon event with a spear _____
6. Baking pan with cuplike molds _____
7. Author of *Future Shock* _____
8. Extra charge the government imposes on cigarettes, alcohol, etc. _____
9. Good facial cream can improve it _____
10. Start of a football game _____
11. Mr. Chips' profession in *Goodbye, Mr. Chips*

    _____
12. Informal term for the former World Trade Center

    _____
13. Browned slice of bread with bits of fruit _____
14. Capital of the Lone Star State _____
15. Where to take a car to watch a movie _____
16. Sea World employee who uses a hoop _____
17. Tender ends of a steak _____
18. You might take one to stop a headache _____

89. SILENT E

Each answer is a familiar two-word phrase in which each word has exactly five letters and ends with a silent E.

Ex. Craft sent out to collect information on planets and such: *Space probe*

1. The president's home _____
2. Permission for a sailor to go on land _____
3. Place to practice shooting _____
4. Fruit drink made by Welch's _____
5. Popular side dish made by Mott's _____
6. In writing, a punctuation mark at the end of what someone says

   _____
7. Exercise of sheer might, as in opening a jammed door

   _____
8. It's less than 90° _____
9. It was won by Jimmy Carter in 2002 and Al Gore in 2007

   _____
10. What a Hopi Indian might perform with a rattler _____
11. An unfocused search is said to be a wild _____
12. Actress who played Mama in the movie *I Remember Mama*

    _____
13. It might have a chalk outline of a body on the ground

    _____
14. Old commerce of the type conducted by the Amistad

    _____
15. Brush with disaster, where you have a narrow escape

    _____
16. Ordinary intelligence in everyday matters _____

90. ARTIFICIAL INTELLIGENCE

Each answer is a compound word or a familiar two-word phrase or name in which the first word has a long A vowel sound and the second word has a long I vowel sound.
Ex. Transportation via Amtrak: *Train ride*

1. The shortest distance between two points

   _____

2. What you use to cut a T-bone _____
3. Manicurist's implement _____
4. Result of an asp's attack _____
5. Informal source of information _____
6. It might make an actor forget his lines _____
7. Something red that shows on the back of a car

   _____

8. Two-wheeler you take off-road _____
9. When kickoff is scheduled at a football stadium

   _____

10. After 11 P.M., say (hyph.) _____
11. Illegal violence against a minority _____
12. Vladimir Nabokov novel _____
13. Eminem movie of 2002 _____
14. Conduit that carries water away _____
15. Astronaut's trip _____
16. Place for a headstone _____
17. According to a saying, they think alike _____

91. TNT

Each answer is a familiar two-word phrase or name in which the first word starts with T and the second word ends with NT.
Ex. Noncommissioned officer rated E-8 in the Army: *Top sergeant*

1. Person who arranges airline tickets for you _____
2. Classroom aide _____
3. Donald Regan headed it for Ronald Reagan _____
4. Hurdles or the 100-meter dash _____
5. Where momentum shifts in a contest _____
6. Copper, iodine, manganese, or molybdenum, e.g., in the human body _____
7. Standard amount for tithing _____
8. Where you might eat sticky rice and food with satay sauce _____
9. Commercial pact to lower tariffs, for example _____
10. Legislative body that sits in Ankara _____
11. What Venus and Serena Williams compete in _____
12. Thomas Lipton, for one _____
13. Rock guitarist famous for "Cat Scratch Fever" _____
14. Its leaves are used to make cigarettes _____
15. Christmas ball or angel for hanging _____
16. "Thou shalt not covet thy neighbor's wife" for Jews and most Protestants _____
17. Game of clues in search of a prize _____
18. _____Ninja Turtles

92. POINT OF VIEW

Each answer is a familiar three-word phrase in which the first word begins with P and the second word is "of."

Ex. What an invading army needs before starting: *Plan of attack*

1. It's at the end of a rainbow _____
2. Noun, verb, or adjective, for example _____
3. What Shylock tried to exact from Antonio in *The Merchant of Venice* _____
4. Title for Charles, in Great Britain _____
5. Old silver coins on the Spanish Main _____
6. Soldier captured by the enemy _____
7. Material used in making ornamental casts _____
8. Location named on a passport _____
9. Something recited in a classroom _____
10. Gilbert and Sullivan operetta _____
11. Logical method involved in ruling out one possibility after another _____
12. What Lot's wife was turned into _____
13. Legal document letting one person represent another _____
14. What you might buy at a Florsheim or Thom McAn store _____
15. What you might give at the Red Cross drive _____
16. Cry from a parliamentarian at a meeting _____
17. Jacques Chirac, formerly _____
18. Feeling of comfort and safety _____
19. Where a ship stops to take on or discharge passengers _____
20. Slang term meaning "easy" _____

93. BABES

Each answer is a familiar two-word phrase or name in which the first word starts with BA and the second word starts with BE.

Ex. The meat in a sloppy joe: *Barbecue beef*

1. Product made by Heinz or B&M _____
2. Small steel roller in a machine _____
3. Wager made over drinks _____
4. Where the parliamentary members who aren't leaders sit in the House of Commons _____
5. Spinoff from AT&T in 1984 _____
6. They make bubbles in a tub _____
7. Old-fashioned term for a pretty woman sunning herself _____
8. Wooden rail that a gymnast performs on _____
9. Stretch of sand protecting a coastline _____
10. Insect that lives under the outer layer of a tree _____
11. Poor conduct or acting up _____
12. A plié, for example, done by a performer in a tutu _____
13. Playboy cover girl who had a longtime relationship with Hugh Hefner _____
14. I-695 in Maryland _____
15. Brand of brew once advertised with a Mitch Miller singalong _____

94. FOR EASTER SUNDAY

Each answer is a familiar two-word phrase or name with the initials E. S.

Ex. Men's grooming item with a cord: *Electric shaver*

1. Nickname for New York _____
2. Central American country _____
3. Venus; or a bygone newspaper in Washington, D.C. _____
4. Curative addition to bath water _____
5. Boy with merit badges _____
6. It shoots a pilot out of a jet _____
7. Respected former public official _____
8. Grades 1–6 _____
9. Something they say not to drink alcohol on _____
10. California condor or Bengal tiger, for example _____
11. What goes between 2+2 and 4 _____
12. Popular sandwich filling _____
13. Classic surfing movie or Beach Boys album _____
14. It's lit in a movie theater _____
15. Geology or geography _____
16. Where the U.N. is in Manhattan _____
17. Comfortable living, figuratively _____
18. Foreign visitor for the school year _____
19. Muffler and tailpipe _____
20. Corporate official's assistant _____

95. CRAWLING WITH ANTS

Each answer is a familiar two-word phrase or name in which the first word ends in AN and the second word starts with T.

Ex. Small baked dessert with nuts: *Pecan tart*

1. Nickname for Boston _____
2. Hiker's path from Georgia to Maine _____
3. Oklahoma before it was Oklahoma _____
4. For a right triangle, $a^2 + b^2 = c^2$ _____
5. Brand of luggage _____
6. Something extremely hard to do _____
7. Card game also called parliament or sevens _____
8. Greenwich _____ _____
9. Welsh poet who wrote "Do Not Go Gentle into That Good Night" _____
10. Zulu, Hottentot, or Tutsi _____
11. Allied armored vehicle in World War II _____
12. Path an egg takes from the ovary _____
13. What a Walk/Don't Walk sign regulates _____
14. *Macbeth* or *Antony and Cleopatra* _____
15. Prestigious college football award _____

96. RDA

Each answer is a familiar two-word phrase or name that contains the consecutive letters RDA.

Ex. The tween years, so it's said: *Awkward age*

1. Engineering feat on the Colorado River _____
2. Highest turnout ever _____
3. Singer Yankovic _____
4. Right not to have soldiers quartered in your home

   _____
5. What an evangelist might call God _____
6. Spanish Surrealist _____
7. Information usually stored in binary code _____
8. Evening event involving eating and music _____
9. Wealthy older man who gives money to an ingénue

   _____
10. Nearly heart-shaped tropical American fruit

    _____
11. The Beatles's *Revolver* or *Rubber Soul* _____
12. An Indian might do it before going into battle

    _____
13. What workers celebrate in early September

    _____
14. Method in psychoanalysis where someone says
    a term and you say whatever jumps to mind

    _____

97. S OF THE S

Each answer is a familiar four-word phrase in which the first word starts with S and the second and third words are "of the."

Ex. A small, silly error in speech: *Slip of the tongue*

1. Capricorn, Leo, Aquarius, etc. _____
2. Hot dish before an entree that a waitress announces specially _____
3. Subject for an annual presidential address in Congress _____
4. Congressional bigwig _____
5. Cabinet officer in charge of monetary matters _____
6. Area marked off with police tape _____
7. What you say when someone you've been talking about suddenly shows up _____
8. Wee, small hours, as sung about by the Five Satins with "In" _____
9. Mexico, to the United States _____
10. Nickname for a camel _____
11. Jodie Foster/Anthony Hopkins film from 1991, with *The* _____
12. Disney musical based on the Uncle Remus stories _____
13. Sudden time when you decide to do something _____
14. TV game show in which contestants won the right to "buy" prizes for very little money (1970s–'80s) _____
15. Person or group representing the most dependable and steadfast elements of society _____
16. Area near a spine's base _____
17. Foundation of Darwinian theory _____

98. SAVINGS AND LOAN

Each answer is a familiar two-word phrase or name with the initials S. L.

Ex. Petulant type: *Sore loser*

1. How a deaf person communicates _____
2. Nobody doesn't like her, in a slogan _____
3. Nathaniel Hawthorne novel, with *The* _____
4. Sailor's balance on a ship _____
5. What every cloud is said to have _____
6. On many roads, 65 m.p.h. _____
7. Painting of a bowl of fruit, for example _____
8. It can tan you indoors _____
9. Long car used by celebrities _____
10. T-bar _____
11. Rank above sergeant major in the army _____
12. Tchaikovsky ballet _____
13. Brutal taskmaster in *Uncle Tom's Cabin* _____
14. African country whose capital is Freetown _____
15. City famous for its Gateway Arch _____

99. JUST SO

Each answer is a familiar two-word phrase or name with the initials S. O.

Ex. Part of an executive's compensation: *Stock option*

1. Afternoon TV serial _____
2. Enthusiastic response for a speaker _____
3. Large group that plays classical music _____
4. Plantation owner in *Gone With the Wind* _____
5. Unmarried romantic partner, more serious than just a boyfriend or girlfriend _____
6. Breakfast dish having a filling of green pepper, onion, and tomato _____
7. It begins: "On my honor I will do my best / To do my duty to God and my country . . ." _____
8. Barn bird with a harsh cry _____
9. Playful marine animal _____
10. Midway between noon and midnight _____
11. The mineral argentite _____
12. Bunkum or hooey that a traveling salesman might try to sell you _____
13. Quadrennial event that includes gymnastics and track and field _____
14. Person who routes incoming telephone calls _____
15. Before a doctor convinces you to have an operation, you should seek this _____
16. Continuation of the film title that begins *2001* (with *A*)
_____

100. EXTRA HELPING OF T

Each answer is a word or a familiar phrase containing three or more syllables in which each syllable begins with the letter T.

Ex. Not definite: *Tentative*

1. One who snitches _____
2. Completely avoid alcohol _____
3. Game with X's and O's _____
4. One whose job is to sample foods for flavor _____
5. "Peter Piper picked a peck of pickled peppers," for example _____
6. Being in direct opposition, as fighters _____
7. With lyrics adapted from the Book of Ecclesiastes, the 1965 #1 hit for the Byrds _____
8. Ore-Ida Foods brand name _____
9. Nathaniel Hawthorne book _____
10. Scold for committing an error _____
11. Person who makes a will _____
12. Having been proved valid over many years _____
13. Seesaw _____
14. Sound of a grandfather clock _____
15. The time 11:38 (five syllables) _____
16. Lines after "A tutor who tooted a flute . . ." (nine syllables) _____

ANSWERS TO PUZZLES

1. P'S AND CLUES

1. Pawn shop
2. Pea soup
3. Potato chip
4. Pistol-whip
5. Postnasal drip
6. Pirate ship
7. Postage stamp
8. Pork chop
9. Pop top
10. Pickup
11. Power trip
12. Pole lamp
13. Poker chip
14. Pit stop
15. Pop group

2. DOUBLE CURVE

1. Social Security
2. Simon Says
3. Soy sauce
4. Super Sunday
5. Sixth sense
6. San Salvador
7. Sales slip
8. Sad Sack
9. Safe sex
10. Sixty seconds
11. "Sunrise, Sunset"
12. Solar system
13. *Sesame Street*
14. Suspended sentence
15. Submarine sandwich
16. Sam Spade
17. *Silent Spring*
18. Status symbol
19. Si si, señor
20. Selective Service System

3. BB'S

1. Boo-boo
2. Bobby
3. Barbie
4. Bamboo
5. Bombay
6. Bible
7. Baboon
8. Bobbin
9. *Babbitt*
10. Barber
11. Brickbat
12. Bonbon
13. Barbell
14. Bourbon
15. Bellboy
16. Beanbag
17. Bareback
18. Blackbeard
19. Bumblebee
20. Blow-by-blow

4. BIG TEASE

1. Top ten
2. Tow truck
3. Tray table
4. Turkey trot
5. Two terms
6. Table tennis
7. Tank top
8. Title track
9. Tag team
10. Tea table
11. Tie tack
12. Toilet training
13. Train tracks
14. Test tube
15. Terrible twos

5. WORDS TO THE Y'S

1. Yale University
2. "Yesterday"
3. Yearly
4. Yoknapatawpha County
5. Yellowbelly
6. Yeomanry
7. *You Don't Say*
8. Yukon Territory
9. *Yankee Doodle Dandy*
10. Yevgeny
11. "You've come a long way, baby"
12. "Your majesty"
13. Yea or nay
14. Yummy
15. Yours truly

6. DOUBLE W

1. Snow White
2. Glowworm
3. New World
4. Window washer
5. Slow-witted
6. Throw weight
7. Andrew Wyeth
8. *Rainbow Warrior*
9. Bowwow
10. Saw wood
11. Common-law wife
12. Plowwright
13. New wave
14. Woodrow Wilson

7. LL FOR YOUR BEAN

1. William Tell
2. Roll call
3. Jelly Roll
4. Yellowbelly
5. Volleyball
6. Dillydally (or shilly-shally)
7. Ill will
8. Illegally
9. Bill Cullen
10. Pall Mall
11. Dullsville
12. *Hello, Dolly!*
13. All Hallows
14. Tell-all
15. Collect call
16. Milli Vanilli
17. Chancellorsville
18. Gallup poll

8. BEGIN, AGAIN

1. Hit the hay
2. Ban the bomb
3. Hark the herald
4. Raise the roof
5. Pound the pavement
6. Below the belt
7. Rule the roost
8. Break the bank
9. Turn the tide
10. Bite the bullet
11. Pull the plug
12. Raid the refrigerator

9. H-HOUR

1. High heels
2. Hear! Hear!
3. Happy holidays
4. *Hee Haw*

5. Haunted house
6. Heavy hitter
7. Hard hat
8. Heavenly hosts
9. Head honcho
10. Heave ho
11. Household hints
12. Harry Houdini
13. "Heartbreak Hotel"
14. Hog heaven
15. "Hip hip hooray!"

10. SPECIAL K

1. Blackjack
2. Cookbook
3. Mukluk
4. Duckwalk
5. Backpack (or rucksack)
6. Knickknack
7. Bookmark
8. Knock-knock
9. Blank check
10. Oak Park
11. Punk rock
12. Clockwork
13. Breakneck
14. Greek Week
15. Shock jock
16. Dick Clark
17. Picklock
18. Think tank

11. GOING CA-CA

1. Cable car
2. Candy cane
3. Calico cat
4. Cattle call
5. Cape Canaveral
6. Cab Calloway
7. *Candid Camera*

8. Card catalogue
9. Carlsbad Caverns
10. Calcium carbonate
11. Carrot cake
12. Cave canem
13. Calling card

12. SECOND STREET

1. Ghost story
2. Rest stop
3. Last stand
4. First strike
5. Guest star
6. Communist state
7. Largest Store
8. *Greatest Story*
9. Rust stain
10. Last straw
11. Dust storm
12. First State
13. Breaststroke

13. PEEPING

1. Pen pals
2. Peace pipe
3. Pet peeve
4. Pea pods
5. Pike's Peak
6. Park Place
7. Puff piece
8. Pepper pot
9. Pill popper
10. Pied Piper
11. Pod people
12. Purple prose
13. Poppy plant
14. Puppet play
15. Prize pupil
16. Paper plate
17. Purple people

14. EASY E'S

1. Green cheese
2. Free speech
3. Queen bee
4. Three feet
5. Fleet Street
6. Bee's knees
7. Beech tree
8. Greek Week
9. Knee-deep
10. Teen queen
11. Greens fee
12. Sheep breed
13. Bee Gees
14. Pee Wee Reese
15. "Wee wee wee"

15. B.C.

1. Hubcap
2. Bobcat
3. Crabcake
4. Lamb chop
5. Rib cage
6. Pub crawl
7. Job Corps
8. Club car
9. Cab Calloway
10. Herb Caen
11. Arab country
12. Verb conjugation
13. Lab coat
14. Bob Costas

16. OOPS

1. Oval Office
2. Olive Oyl
3. One o'clock
4. Osage orange
5. Obey orders
6. Operation Overlord
7. Ole Olsen
8. Ozzy Osborne
9. Old Orchard
10. Offshore oil
11. October one
12. Oath of Office
13. Out of order
14. On one's own
15. Oil of Olay

17. P-NUTS

1. Lamppost
2. Gallup poll
3. Strip poker
4. Stop payment
5. Stepparent
6. Drip pan
7. Deep Purple
8. Slip past
9. Pep pill
10. Top priority
11. Group practice
12. Stamp pad
13. Soup plate
14. Soap pad
15. Snap peas

18. MAMA

1. Math major
2. March Madness
3. Masked man
4. Mayflower Madam
5. Mad magazine
6. Martin Marietta
7. *Marathon Man*
8. Mass market
9. *Mad Max*
10. Marla Maples
11. Mary Magdalene
12. Marcello Mastroianni
13. Marlboro Man
14. Manfred Mann
15. Manassa Mauler
16. Maid Marian

19. HIDDEN LEAD

1. Soapbox
2. Humpback
3. Clipboard
4. Scrapbook
5. Hipbone
6. Cupbearer
7. Shipbuilding
8. Jump ball
9. Lip balm
10. Ketchup bottle (or catsup bottle)
11. Tulip bulbs
12. Soup bone
13. Lampblack
14. Top banana

20. 2-D

1. Salad dressing
2. Speed demon
3. Hard drive (or hard disk)
4. Sled dog
5. Blood drive
6. Blind date
7. Mixed doubles
8. Coed dorm
9. Third degree
10. Round dance
11. "Hound Dog"
12. Dead duck
13. Gold digger
14. Old Dominion
15. Ford dealer
16. Wind direction
17. Card deck
18. Liquid diet
19. Bad dream
20. Good day

21. AA BATTERIES

1. Adam's apple
2. "All aboard!"
3. "Anchors aweigh!"
4. Affirmative action
5. Acute angle
6. Army ants
7. Academy Awards
8. Amino acids
9. Ann Arbor
10. *Advertising Age*
11. American Airlines
12. Arabic alphabet
13. Administrative assistant
14. Addis Ababa

22. DISTRICT OF COLUMBIA

1. Dog collar
2. Dunce cap
3. Drain cleaner
4. Dixie cup
5. Day care
6. Deck chair
7. Direct current
8. Dining car
9. Double cross
10. Drama critic
11. Depth charge
12. Desk calendar
13. Diplomatic corps
14. Disorderly conduct
15. "Divine Comedy"
16. Distress call
17. Drug czar
18. Dress code
19. Dry cleaner
20. Digital camera

23. EEK!

1. Easter egg
2. Electric eel
3. Emergency exit
4. Eastern Europe
5. Evil empire
6. Energy-efficient
7. Egyptian embassy
8. Entrance exam
9. En Español
10. Elephant's ears
11. Evening edition
12. Elementary education
13. English essayist
14. Emilio Estevez
15. Electrical engineer
16. "Extra! Extra!"

24. ING-GOTS

1. Boxing gloves
2. Wedding gown
3. Chewing gum
4. Passing grade
5. Bowling Green
6. Letting go
7. Shooting gallery
8. Crossing guard
9. Starting gate
10. Laughing gas
11. *Crying Game*
12. "Amazing Grace"
13. Looking glass
14. Running gag
15. Landing gear

25. PH FACTOR

1. Panama hat
2. Pith helmet
3. Plow horse
4. Pinch hitter
5. Poker hand
6. Patrick Henry
7. Pearl Harbor
8. Purple Heart
9. Public housing
10. Plaza Hotel
11. Procol Harum
12. *Prizzi's Honor*
13. Publishing house
14. Pizza Hut

26. PJ'S

1. Plain Jane
2. Pickle jar
3. Practical joke
4. Pope John
5. Poetic justice
6. Pearl Jam
7. Prune juice
8. Pea jacket
9. Paint job
10. *Pal Joey*
11. *Petticoat Junction*
12. Pizza joint
13. Puddle jumper
14. Petroleum jelly

27. HOT SPOT

1. Honor student
2. Hair salon
3. Hardware store
4. High society
5. *Hollywood Squares*
6. Ham sandwich
7. Hula skirt
8. Hoosier State
9. Horse show
10. Hot sauce
11. Hockey stick
12. Hunger strike
13. Head start
14. Home stretch

28. CB TALK

1. Crystal ball
2. Cat burglar
3. Carte blanche
4. Coke bottles
5. Contract bridge
6. Coffee break
7. Cabin boy
8. Comic book
9. Cordon bleu
10. Cutting board
11. Corned beef
12. Cocoa butter
13. *College Bowl*
14. Color blindness
15. Combat boots
16. Credit bureau
17. Catcher's box
18. Continental breakfast

29. LIPLOCK

1. Looseleaf
2. Longlegs
3. Lovelorn
4. Landlocked
5. Lemon-lime
6. Lily-livered
7. Lackluster
8. Landlord or landlady
9. Lowlife
10. Longleaf
11. Lend-Lease
12. Linkletter
13. Limelight
14. Landlubber

30. POSTSCRIPT

1. Dipstick
2. Hopscotch
3. Pipsqueak
4. Ripsaw (or whipsaw)
5. Sapsucker
6. Topspin
7. Campsite
8. Lipstick
9. Deep-six
10. Slapstick
11. Soupspoon
12. Stepson
13. Cheapskate
14. Sheepskin
15. Sweepstakes

31. "A" THERE

1. Straight face
2. Freight train
3. Space Age (or Space Race)
4. Rain date
5. Great Dane
6. Chain mail
7. Trade name
8. Bake sale
9. Weight gain
10. Eight days
11. Snail's pace
12. Brain waves
13. Great Slave Lake

32. THE LAST SHALL BE FIRST

1. Lake Erie
2. Flat tire
3. Foul line
4. Swim meet
5. Rush hour
6. Left turn
7. Jane Eyre
8. Half fare
9. Post time
10. Sand dune
11. Test tube
12. Hard drug
13. Dead duck
14. Plus sign
15. Sore eyes

33. THAT'S SOMETHING

1. Sore thumb
2. Second thought
3. Stone's throw
4. "Strike three"
5. Speech therapy
6. Set theory
7. Strom Thurmond
8. Summer theater
9. Spring thaw
10. Surgical thread
11. September third
12. Six thousand
13. Sneak thief
14. Seeing things

34. EAST SIDE

1. Easter parade
2. Egg white
3. Entry fee
4. Elbow grease
5. Emerald Isle
6. Empire State
7. Exhaust pipe
8. Exchange rate
9. Eau Claire
10. Emergency brake
11. "En garde"
12. Escape clause
13. Eskimo Pie
14. Executive privilege
15. Evergreen tree
16. End zone

35. ON THE DL

1. Detroit Lions
2. Dalai Lama
3. Daddy longlegs
4. Dead language
5. Dean's list
6. Dirty look
7. Dotted line
8. Driver's license
9. Dirty laundry
10. Dog leg
11. Dance lesson
12. Doctor Livingstone
13. Diamond Lil
14. Designer label
15. Divorce lawyer

36. THE WB

1. Wine bottle
2. Wonder Bread
3. World Book
4. Warm blood
5. Wet blanket
6. Window box
7. Worry beads
8. Wading bird
9. Waikiki Beach
10. Water Bearer
11. Wooly Bully
12. War bride
13. Washington's birthday
14. Weather bureau
15. Web browser
16. Wild Bill
17. Wiffle ball
18. West Bank
19. Wedding bells
20. Welcome back!

37. ARMS CACHE

1. Bar mitzvah
2. Bear market
3. Handlebar mustache
4. Lunar module
5. Near miss
6. Popular music
7. Sugar maple
8. Cigar maker
9. Ear muffs
10. War memorial
11. Oscar Mayer
12. Dollar menu
13. Linear measure
14. Star map
15. Nuclear material
16. "Dear me!"

38. AT THE HEART OF THE MATTER

1. Sack race
2. Leap year
3. Barnyard
4. Dead heat
5. Golf hole
6. Chop shot
7. Sandbank
8. Mainsail
9. Karl Marx
10. Wish list
11. Fall sale
12. Grey area
13. Firebird
14. Boatload
15. Pool room

39. ROW YOUR BOAT

1. Brooks Brothers
2. Wrought iron
3. Broken promise
4. Proving ground
5. Drove around
6. Cross promotion
7. Brook trout
8. Brownie troop
9. Ground erosion
10. Gross profit
11. Prove wrong
12. Iron Cross
13. Brooklyn trolley
14. "Drop trou"

40. LEFT AND RIGHT

1. Little Rock
2. Life raft
3. Lightning rod
4. Lip reader
5. Little Richard
6. Linda Ronstadt
7. Lionel Richie
8. Leann Rimes
9. Light red
10. Lime rickey
11. Lead role
12. Law review
13. Lab rat
14. Luggage rack
15. Locker room
16. Last resort

41. END TO END

1. Little League
2. Trade deficit
3. Ghost story
4. Maple leaf

5. Horse sense
6. Space center
7. Prime meridian
8. Computer error
9. Tear around
10. Angela Lansbury
11. San Antonio
12. Rest stop
13. English sheepdog

42. WORD PLAY

1. West Point
2. Water pistol
3. Wanted poster
4. Warsaw Pact
5. Widow's peak
6. Wet paint
7. Wax paper
8. Wall plug
9. Wolf pack
10. Word puzzle
11. Wedding planner
12. Winter Palace
13. Waiting period
14. Whipping post
15. Wind power
16. World premiere

43. FOR PROS

1. Plymouth Rock
2. Powder room
3. Paper route
4. Pot roast
5. Pitched roof
6. Purple rose
7. Paint roller
8. Piano roll
9. Port Royal
10. Punk rocker
11. Private road
12. Pitching rotation
13. President Roosevelt

14. Pat Robertson
15. Paul Robeson
16. Pete Rose

44. LET'S GO!

1. Low gear
2. Life guard
3. Lip gloss
4. Los Gatos
5. Long green
6. Lady Godiva
7. Lake Geneva
8. Landing gear
9. Laughing gas
10. Looking glass
11. Legal guardian
12. Local government
13. Lieutenant governor
14. Land grant
15. Lead guitar
16. Leaded gasoline
17. Loaded gun
18. Love god

45. M&MS

1. Drum major
2. Skim milk
3. Swim meet
4. *Phantom Menace*
5. Freedom March
6. Jim Morrison
7. Tom Mix
8. Sam Malone
9. *From Mars*
10. Quantum mechanics
11. Sodium monoxide
12. Farm machinery
13. Team mascot
14. Thom McAn
15. William McKinley

46. GOOD THINKING!

1. Guinea pig
2. Goose egg
3. Global warming
4. Gas rationing
5. Greek flag
6. Glass blowing
7. Gift wrapping
8. Grab bag
9. Grade crossing
10. "Git along"
11. *Gold Bug*
12. G String
13. Guide dog
14. Gone fishing

47. ALL ABOUT ME

1. Mount Everest
2. Middle East
3. *Mister Ed*
4. Medical examiner
5. *Morning Edition*
6. Managing editor
7. Mechanical engineer
8. Montreal Expo
9. Manila envelope
10. Main event
11. Mixed emotions
12. *Midnight Express*
13. Modern English
14. "My eye!"
15. Mental exercise

48. PLAYING LPS

1. License plate
2. Lily pad
3. Lake Placid
4. Law professor
5. Labor Party
6. Low point

7. Life preserver
8. Lesson plan
9. Lincoln penny
10. Lord's prayer
11. Launch pad
12. Liquid paper
13. *Little Prince*
14. Love potion
15. Laser printer
16. Labor pains
17. List price
18. Last place

49. CONCEALED LEGS

1. Bubble gum
2. Whole grain
3. Battle ground
4. Jungle gym
5. Durable goods
6. Yale graduate
7. Staple gun
8. *Cable Guy*
9. Estelle Getty
10. Miracle-Gro
11. Tattletale gray
12. Table game
13. Flammable gas (or inflammable gas)
14. Missile gap
15. Idle gossip
16. "Gobble gobble"

50. SIX-POINTERS

1. Tap dance
2. Test drive
3. Tone deafness
4. Tooth decay
5. Telephone directory
6. Ten days
7. Tax deduction
8. *Taxi Driver*

9. Technical difficulties
10. Turkish delight
11. T'ang dynasty
12. Top dog
13. Tongue depressor
14. *Tin Drum*
15. Tasmanian devil
16. Teapot Dome

51. NEW AT HEART

1. One way
2. Stone wall
3. Rhine wine
4. Paine Webber
5. Lone wolf
6. Machine-wash
7. Joanne Woodward
8. Maxene Waters
9. Medicine woman
10. Feminine wiles
11. Engine wear
12. Mine workers
13. Telephone wire
14. Done with

52. LOS ANGELES

1. Liberal arts
2. Latin America
3. Legal age
4. Local anesthesia
5. Liquid assets
6. Late afternoon
7. Left arm
8. LaGuardia airport
9. Louis Armstrong
10. Lew Alcindor
11. Light artillery
12. Love apple
13. Lhasa apso
14. Literary agent
15. Long ago

53. TUTEES

1. Taste test
2. Straight ticket
3. Cotton State
4. Sitting target
5. Cigarette butt
6. District attorney
7. Static electricity
8. Student assistant
9. Abstract thought
10. Identity theft
11. Kitty litter
12. Northwest Territories
13. Street theater
14. Test pattern
15. State Department

54. SPLIT ENDS

1. Seven days
2. Open door
3. Batten down
4. Frozen daiquiri
5. Golden Delicious
6. Sudden death
7. Stephen Douglas
8. Maureen Dowd
9. Chicken dog
10. Magen David
11. Queen dowager
12. Ten Downing
13. Kitchen drawer
14. Allen Drury
15. Ellen Degeneres
16. Green Day
17. Häagen-Dazs

55. POSTSCRIPT II

1. Stop sign
2. Chop suey
3. Soap suds
4. Flip side

5. Jump suit
6. Lump sum
7. Prep school
8. Leap second
9. Warp speed
10. Deep space
11. Friendship Seven
12. Rap session
13. Strip search
14. Stump speech
15. Hoop skirt
16. Shrimp scampi

56. OVERTIME

1. Old Testament
2. Oil tanker
3. Oak tree
4. Oregon Trail
5. Organ transplant
6. Operating table
7. Oxygen tent
8. *Our Town*
9. Oliver Twist
10. Olympic torch
11. Oral test
12. Ohio Turnpike
13. October Twelfth
14. Observation tower
15. Oakland Tribune
16. Oven temperature

57. MASTER OF CEREMONY

1. Alarm clock
2. Mushroom cloud
3. Graham cracker
4. Broom closet
5. Cream cheese
6. Vacuum cleaner
7. Museum curator
8. Clam chowder
9. Gym class

10. Tom Collins
11. Sodium chloride
12. Film clip
13. Stem cell
14. Storm cellar
15. Warm clothes
16. Jim Carrey
17. William Cody
18. Drum corps

58. SUPERSONIC

1. Chess tournament
2. Bess Truman
3. Cordless telephone
4. Miss Texas
5. Express train
6. Brass tacks
7. Class trip
8. Fitness trainer
9. Stress test
10. Boss Tweed
11. Mass transit
12. Bass trombone
13. Business traveler
14. Tess Trueheart
15. Mattress tag

59. THE SHORT AND THE LONG OF IT

1. Crabcake
2. Clambake
3. Brand name
4. Rat race
5. Lamb's tail
6. Grass stain
7. Crankcase
8. Rag trade
9. Backstage
10. Fan mail
11. Handshake
12. Hangnail

13. Dan Quayle
14. Ham steak
15. Gas main
16. Bran flakes
17. Craps game
18. Pass/fail
19. Bad taste
20. Fast break

60. STP

1. First person
2. Best Picture
3. List price
4. Test pattern
5. West Point
6. Exhaust pipe
7. Vest pocket
8. Past participle
9. Rest period
10. Chest protector
11. Forest primeval
12. Oldest profession
13. Northwest Passage
14. Communist Party
15. Compost pile
16. Last place

61. INSIDE THE O.R.

1. Puerto Rico
2. Navajo rug
3. Cargo room
4. Leo Rosten
5. Diego Rivera
6. *Tobacco Road*
7. *Casino Royale*
8. Ohio River
9. Video rental
10. Cameo role
11. Tokyo Rose
12. Piano roll

13. Photo retoucher
14. Camino Real
15. Pro rata
16. "Go Redskins!"

62. REGISTERED NURSE

1. Real name
2. Roman numeral
3. Royal Navy
4. Right now
5. Republican nomination
6. Ralph Nader
7. Robin's nest
8. Round number
9. Romance novel
10. Red nose (or runny nose)
11. Radio network
12. Ricky Nelson
13. Richard Nixon
14. Rusty nail
15. Ransom note

63. FM STATION

1. Fan mail
2. Filet mignon
3. Flea market
4. Flour mill
5. Folding money
6. Free market
7. Face mask
8. Flying machine
9. Folk music
10. Fort McHenry
11. Fu Manchu
12. First Monday
13. Fannie Mae
14. Family medicine
15. Fire marshal
16. Foot massage

17. Foreign minister
18. Full monty

64. A TO B

1. Lima bean
2. Prima ballerina
3. Sofa bed
4. Ouija board
5. Opera buff
6. Panda bear
7. Aurora borealis
8. Plea bargain
9. Camera bag
10. Santa Barbara
11. Tampa Bay
12. Fiesta Bowl
13. Atlanta Braves
14. Flea bite
15. Polka band
16. Encyclopedia Britannica
17. Daytona Beach
18. Sea breeze

65. SEPTEMBER

1. License plate
2. Goose pimples
3. Surprise party
4. Rose petal
5. Noise pollution
6. Grease pencil
7. Chinese premier
8. Pease porridge
9. Cheese puffs
10. Mouse pad
11. Primrose path
12. Blaise Pascal
13. *Melrose Place*
14. Lacrosse player
15. Reverse psychology

66. LOOKING U.P.

1. United Press
2. Upright piano
3. Union Pacific
4. Upper Peninsula
5. Under par
6. Units place
7. Unusual punishment
8. University press
9. Utility pole
10. Umbrella policy
11. Universal Pictures
12. Underarm perspiration
13. Uranium plant
14. Ukulele player
15. Unsalted peanuts

67. SEE WHAT I.C.

1. Ice cream
2. Internal combustion
3. Irish coffee
4. Iron Curtain
5. Ivory Coast
6. Indian corn
7. Insurance company
8. Immaculate conception
9. Inferiority complex
10. Intensive care
11. Inspector Clouseau
12. Imogene Coca
13. Integral calculus
14. "I, Claudius"
15. Instant camera
16. Index card
17. Interstate commerce

68. NET HOLDINGS

1. Fine-tooth(ed)
2. Pine tree
3. Phone tag
4. Plane ticket
5. Maine Turnpike
6. Stone tablets
7. Canine tooth
8. Fortune teller
9. Scalene triangle
10. Acetylene torch
11. Gasoline tax
12. Bone-tired
13. Firestone tire(s)
14. Engine trouble
15. Propane tank
16. Shoshone tribe
17. Spine-tingling
18. Nine-tenths
19. Wine taster
20. Champagne toast

69. ESSEN

1. "Silent Night"
2. Serial number
3. Swedish Nightingale
4. Safety net
5. Sour note
6. Stiff neck
7. Second nature
8. Spiral nebula
9. Sea nymph
10. Stage name
11. Singing Nun
12. Sam Neill
13. Snub nose
14. Silver nitrate
15. Sweet nothings
16. St. Nicholas

70. O. H.?

1. Open house
2. Office hours
3. One hundred
4. *Other Half*
5. Oral history
6. Oliver Hardy
7. Oscar Hammerstein
8. Orrin Hatch
9. "Over here!"
10. Outer Hebrides
11. On hand
12. Oh Henry!
13. Old Hickory
14. Opera hat
15. Olympic's host

71. HA!

1. Hearing aid
2. *Home Alone*
3. Honest Abe
4. Handy Andy
5. Heart attack
6. Heir apparent
7. Hot air
8. House arrest
9. Hydrochloric acid
10. Honda Accord
11. Ham actor
12. Hells Angels
13. Horatio Alger
14. Hebrew alphabet
15. Handwriting analysis
16. *High Anxiety*

72. I.M.ING

1. Ice machine
2. Iron Mike
3. Indian moccasin
4. Imelda Marcos
5. Iris Murdoch
6. Illegal motion
7. *Invisible Man*
8. Inquiring minds
9. Inner Mongolia
10. Instruction manual
11. Imperial margarine
12. In-flight movie
13. Inboard motor
14. Involuntary manslaughter
15. In memoriam
16. "I'm melting"

73. P.O. BOX

1. Police officer
2. Pacific Ocean
3. Presidential Oath
4. Peter O'Toole
5. Pipe organ
6. Peace offering
7. Public opinion
8. Private ownership
9. Poison oak
10. Pit orchestra
11. Puffed Oats
12. Pecking order
13. Pearl oyster
14. Peanut oil
15. Page one

74. A/C

1. Appeals Court
2. Attaché case
3. Armored car
4. Advice column
5. Aircraft carrier
6. Alarm clock
7. Algebra class
8. Alley cat
9. Amicus curiae
10. Animal crackers
11. Area code

12. Agatha Christie
13. Arab country
14. Arms control
15. Alternating current
16. Albert Camus
17. Andrew Carnegie
18. Appointment calendar

75. ALTERNATIVES

1. Short story
2. North Korea
3. Fort Worth
4. Organ donor
5. Morning glory
6. Order form
7. World record
8. Horse doctor
9. Sports editor
10. George Orwell
11. Bjorn Borg
12. Victor Borge
13. Portland, Oregon
14. Tora Bora
15. Aurora borealis
16. Former Mayor
17. Word for word

76. KP DUTY

1. Cockpit
2. Backpack
3. Stockpile
4. Neckpiece
5. Bookplate
6. Duckpins
7. Shockproof
8. Pickpocket
9. Porkpie
10. Crackpot
11. Workplace
12. Rockport

13. Chickpeas
14. Checkpoint

77. RH FACTOR

1. Red herring
2. Rest home
3. Right hand
4. Road hog
5. Robin Hood
6. Rocking horse
7. Rubber hose
8. Rosh Hashanah
9. Royal Highness
10. *Rocky Horror*
11. Relative humidity
12. Round hole
13. Rush hour
14. Record holder
15. Rock Hudson
16. Rex Harrison
17. Rita Hayworth
18. Ron Howard
19. Riverdale High
20. Random House

78. ALL EARS

1. House arrest
2. Escape artist
3. Tone arm
4. Cave art
5. Tempe, Arizona
6. Plate armor
7. Magazine article
8. Picture archive
9. Late arrival
10. Roseanne Arnold
11. Lucie Arnaz
12. Eve Arden
13. Eddie Arcaro
14. Side arm
15. Chinese army
16. Game arcade

79. C.I. TOLD YOU SO

1. Coney Island
2. Cleveland Indians
3. Curling iron
4. Car insurance
5. Chrysler Imperial
6. Column inch
7. Chief inspector
8. Chocolate icing
9. Current issue
10. Central Intelligence
11. Caller ID
12. Collector's item
13. Card index
14. Compound interest
15. Cottage industry
16. "Cheese it!"

80. VERY FINE

1. Vote fraud
2. Valley Forge
3. Vanilla flavor(ing)
4. Vanity Fair
5. Virgin forest
6. Vegetable fat
7. Victoria Falls
8. Vicente Fox
9. Velvet Fog
10. Volume four
11. Volunteer fireman
12. Venus fly-trap
13. Vietnamese flag
14. Violin family
15. Verse form
16. V formation

81. FOR VETERAN'S DAY

1. Love triangle
2. Drive time

3. Shrove Tuesday
4. Slave trade
5. Dave Thomas
6. Five times
7. Adhesive tape
8. Digestive tract
9. Jive talk
10. Nerve tissue
11. Native tongue
12. Recessive trait
13. Live television
14. Conservative talk
15. Stove Top
16. Olive tree

82. BRR!

1. Brick road
2. Brer Rabbit
3. Bragging rights
4. Breathing room
5. Brown rice
6. Bright red
7. Broken record
8. Breakfast room
9. Brake repairman
10. Bridal registry
11. Bronx River
12. Brooks Robinson
13. Breeder reactor

83. OPERATING ROOM

1. Oak Ridge
2. Oral Roberts
3. Oven rack
4. Ohio River
5. Oil rig
6. Organ recital
7. Onion rings
8. Oriental rug
9. Orville Redenbacher
10. Otis Redding

11. *Oedipus Rex*
12. Oakland Raiders
13. Opinion research
14. October Revolution
15. Organized religion
16. Orange rind
17. Octane rating
18. Original recipe

84. INSIDE WARNER BROS.

1. Rowboat
2. Sawbuck
3. Crowbar
4. Newborn
5. Lowbrow
6. Cowboy
7. Yellowbellied
8. Snowboarding
9. Screwball
10. Shadowbox
11. Narrowband
12. Strawberry
13. Showbiz
14. Drawbridge
15. Browbeat
16. Jawbreaker

85. NC-17

1. News conference
2. Nose cone
3. National convention
4. Night court
5. Nudist colony
6. Number cruncher
7. Nouvelle cuisine
8. No contest
9. Noël Coward
10. Nicolas Cage
11. Natalie Cole
12. Ninth Commandment
13. Norman Conquest

14. "New Colossus"
15. Nestlé Crunch
16. Neutral corner
17. Nail clipper

86. LONG ISLAND

1. Little Italy
2. Life insurance
3. Large intestine (or lower intestine)
4. Lafayette, Indiana
5. Leg irons
6. Lemon ice
7. Lethal injection
8. Line item
9. Low income
10. Legally intoxicated
11. Lee Iacocca
12. Latin instructor
13. Love interest
14. Leather interior
15. Lincoln's Inaugural

87. FOR FATHER'S DAY

1. Flight deck
2. Floppy disk
3. Fifth Dimension
4. French dressing
5. Front door
6. Frozen daiquiri
7. Five dollars
8. Film director
9. Fashion designer
10. Financial district
11. Fad diet
12. Fair Deal
13. Fairy dust
14. Female deer
15. Ford dealer
16. Foot doctor

17. Fire drill
18. Fireworks display

88. INTERESTING

1. Train track(s)
2. Brain trust
3. Hairpin turn
4. Mountain Time
5. Javelin throw
6. Muffin tin
7. Alvin Toffler
8. Sin tax
9. Skin tone (or skin texture)
10. Coin toss
11. Latin teacher
12. Twin Towers
13. Raisin toast
14. Austin, Texas
15. Drive-in theater
16. Dolphin trainer
17. Sirloin tips
18. Aspirin tablet

89. SILENT E

1. White House
2. Shore leave
3. Rifle range
4. Grape juice
5. Apple sauce
6. Close quote
7. Brute force
8. Acute angle
9. Peace Prize
10. Snake dance
11. Goose chase
12. Irene Dunne
13. Crime scene
14. Slave trade
15. Close shave
16. Horse sense

90. ARTIFICIAL INTELLIGENCE

1. Straight line
2. Steak knife
3. Nail file
4. Snake bite
5. Grapevine
6. Stage fright
7. Brake light (or tail light)
8. Trail bike
9. Game time
10. Late-night
11. Hate crime
12. *Pale Fire*
13. *Eight Mile*
14. Drainpipe
15. Space flight
16. Grave site
17. Great minds

91. TNT

1. Travel agent
2. Teaching assistant
3. Treasury Department
4. Track event
5. Turning point
6. Trace element
7. Ten percent
8. Thai restaurant
9. Trade agreement
10. Turkish parliament
11. Tennis tournament
12. Tea merchant
13. Ted Nugent
14. Tobacco plant
15. Tree ornament
16. Tenth commandment
17. Treasure hunt
18. Teenage Mutant

92. POINT OF VIEW

1. Pot of gold
2. Part of speech
3. Pound of flesh
4. Prince of Wales
5. Pieces of eight
6. Prisoner of war
7. Plaster of Paris
8. Place of birth
9. Pledge of Allegiance
10. *Pirates of Penzance*
11. Process of elimination
12. Pillar of salt
13. Power of attorney
14. Pair of shoes
15. Pint of blood
16. Point of order
17. President of France
18. Peace of mind
19. Port of call
20. Piece of cake

93. BABES

1. Baked beans
2. Ball bearing
3. Bar bet
4. Back bench
5. Baby Bell
6. Bath beads
7. Bathing beauty
8. Balance beam
9. Barrier beach
10. Bark beetle
11. Bad behavior
12. Ballet bend
13. Barbi Benton

14. Baltimore Beltway
15. Ballantine beer

94. FOR EASTER SUNDAY

1. Empire State
2. El Salvador
3. Evening Star
4. Epsom salts
5. Eagle scout
6. Ejector seat
7. Elder statesman
8. Elementary school
9. Empty stomach
10. Endangered species
11. Equal sign
12. Egg salad
13. *Endless Summer*
14. Exit sign
15. Earth science
16. East Side
17. Easy street
18. Exchange student
19. Exhaust system
20. Executive secretary

95. CRAWLING WITH ANTS

1. Bean Town
2. Appalachian Trail
3. Indian Territory
4. Pythagorean theorem
5. American Tourister
6. Herculean task
7. Fan tan
8. Mean Time
9. Dylan Thomas
10. African tribe
11. Sherman tank

12. Fallopian tube
13. Pedestrian traffic
14. Shakespearean tragedy
15. Heisman Trophy

96. RDA

1. Hoover Dam
2. Record attendance
3. Weird Al
4. Third Amendment
5. Lord Almighty
6. Salvador Dali
7. Computer data (or user data)
8. Dinner dance
9. Sugar daddy
10. Custard apple
11. Record album
12. War dance
13. Labor Day
14. Word association

97. S OF THE S

1. Sign of the zodiac
2. Soup of the day
3. State of the Union
4. Speaker of the House
5. Secretary of the Treasury
6. Scene of the crime
7. Speak of the devil
8. "Still of the Night"
9. South of the border
10. Ship of the desert
11. *Silence of the Lambs*
12. *Song of the South*
13. Spur of the moment
14. *Sale of the Century*

15. Salt of the earth
16. Small of the back
17. Survival of the fittest

98. SAVINGS AND LOAN

1. Sign language
2. Sara Lee
3. *Scarlet Letter*
4. Sea legs
5. Silver lining
6. Speed limit
7. Still life
8. Sun lamp
9. Stretch limo
10. Ski lift
11. Second lieutenant
12. *Swan Lake*
13. Simon Legree
14. Sierra Leone
15. St. Louis

99. JUST SO

1. Soap opera
2. Standing ovation
3. Symphony orchestra
4. Scarlett O'Hara
5. Significant other
6. Spanish omelet
7. Scout oath
8. Screech owl
9. Sea otter
10. Six o'clock
11. Silver ore
12. Snake oil
13. Summer Olympics
14. Switchboard operator
15. Second opinion
16. *Space Odyssey*

100. EXTRA HELPING OF T

1. Tattletale
2. Teetotal
3. Tic-tac-toe
4. Taste tester
5. Tongue twister
6. Toe to toe
7. "Turn! Turn! Turn!"
8. Tater Tots
9. *Twice-Told Tales*
10. Take to task
11. Testator
12. Time-tested
13. Teeter-totter
14. Tick-tock, tick-tock
15. Twenty-two to twelve
16. Tried to tutor two tooters to toot